MACROBIUS, OR PHILOSOPHY, SCIENCE AND LETTERS IN THE YEAR 400

MACROBIUS

OR

PHILOSOPHY, SCIENCE AND LETTERS IN THE YEAR 400

BY

THOMAS WHITTAKER

AUTHOR OF *THE NEO-PLATONISTS*

CAMBRIDGE

AT THE UNIVERSITY PRESS

1923

CAMBRIDGE
UNIVERSITY PRESS

University Printing House, Cambridge CB2 8BS, United Kingdom

Cambridge University Press is part of the University of Cambridge.

It furthers the University's mission by disseminating knowledge in the pursuit of education, learning and research at the highest international levels of excellence.

www.cambridge.org
Information on this title: www.cambridge.org/9781107450974

First published 1923
First paperback edition 2014

A catalogue record for this publication is available from the British Library

ISBN 978-1-107-45097-4 Paperback

PREFACE

I HAVE attempted in this short book to give some account of a philosopher and man of letters who deserved better treatment than he has for some time received. If he was not a writer or thinker of the first order, he had at any rate a coherent doctrine, and the claim, which he modestly makes for himself, to have impressed on what he borrowed an individual Latin style, cannot be gainsaid. Most writers of later antiquity were compilers; but there are two kinds of compilation —books written with heads and without. Of the latter kind, the *Lives of the Philosophers* by Diogenes Laertius is an example. It has been described by Prof. Burnet as a scrap-book, which "has not been digested or composed by any single mind at all." Superficially, a remark of the latest editor of Sextus Empiricus (in the Teubner Series), expressing the fear that nearly everything he gives is collected from other people's writings, may seem to amount to the same thing; but to draw this inference regarding Sextus would be a complete error. There is no set of writings that bears more distinctly than his the mark of a single mind carrying through with conscious mastery a determinate philosophical thought. Macrobius is more obviously a compiler; but he too possessed conscious mastery over his material; and, as I have tried to show, we can still learn much from him both directly and by the study of his place in literature and philosophy.

To English readers, it must always be interesting to remember that Chaucer's account of his own dream in

The Parlement of Foules starts from his reading of the *Somnium Scipionis* with the Commentary of Macrobius, —whose theory of the causes of dreams he closely follows,—and that Dr Johnson gave evidence of the breadth of his early Latin reading by quoting him on his first arrival at Oxford.

Of course the date in the sub-title is not to be taken too precisely. It is not possible to assign the works of Macrobius to any exact year; but there is no doubt that he wrote them near the end of the fourth century.

T. W.

October 1922

P.S. I take this opportunity of correcting an inadvertence and an imperfect reference in *The Neo-Platonists*.

P. 101, l. 11 (2nd ed.). For 'Stoic' read 'Aristotelian.'
" l. 12 " " 'Aristotelian' read 'Stoic.'
P. 189, note (2nd ed.). After *Averroès et l'Averroïsme*, insert 'première partie.'

CONTENTS

Not yore
Agon, hit happed me for to beholde
Upon a boke, was write with lettres olde;
And ther-upon, a certeyn thing to lerne,
The longe day ful faste I radde and yerne.

For out of olde feldes, as men seith,
Cometh al this newe corn fro yeer to yere;
And out of olde bokes, in good feith,
Cometh al this newe science that men lere.
But now to purpos as of this matere—
To rede forth hit gan me so delyte,
That al the day me thoughte but a lyte.

CHAUCER, *The Parlement of Foules.*

The Reverend Dr Adams, who afterwards presided over Pembroke College with universal esteem, told me he was present, and gave me some account of what passed on the night of Johnson's arrival at Oxford.... His figure and manner appeared strange to them; but he behaved modestly, and sat silent, till upon something which occurred in the course of conversation, he suddenly struck in and quoted Macrobius.

BOSWELL'S *Life of Johnson*,
ed. G. Birkbeck Hill, vol. I. p. 59.

MACROBIUS

I

INTRODUCTION

Reading lately the story of Cupid and Psyche in Apuleius, I found myself carried off into a train of allegorising thought in such an easy and apparently spontaneous way that I could not help thinking that Apuleius, in giving form to the myth, was inspired by what Shakespeare calls the prophetic soul of the world. For us moderns, the idea, when once suggested, is very easy to follow; and Apuleius, though he could not of course know exactly, may, in the transitional age of the second century, have had some divination of the future. A brief outline of the train of thought will be a not irrelevant introduction to the present Essay.

In modern times, Apuleius is best known as the author of the *Metamorphoses*, commonly called *The Golden Ass*. In antiquity, his reputation was that of a Platonic philosopher: that he should have deviated into story-telling was thought to be something of a falling-off. He tells us, indeed, in his reply to a charge of magic, that he was accused of being only a pretender to philosophy because he possessed a mirror. Such was the demand for simplicity in the philosophic life that a mirror was hardly permissible to a philosopher except for the sake of science[1]. Used for trimming the hair and beard, it was

[1] Cf. Seneca, *Naturales Quaestiones*, I. 17.

a luxury. And, as late as Boethius, we find the Muses of imaginative literature, when they present themselves as rivals of the severer kind of knowledge, driven from the scene. The distinctive gift of Apuleius was, however, not for science, but for a new kind of literature, in which, after an assiduous training in style that can be traced in his extant works, he produced a masterpiece of exuberant genius of the kind that we have become accustomed to call romantic rather than distinctively classical.

Yet the Platonic philosopher in him always remained; and it was precisely the new drift of return to metaphysics after a period of practical philosophy that produced a delayed efflorescence of new art. The destiny of the world prevented the new impulses in literature from getting free at the time. There was to be a long lapse until, to apply a line of Shelley, the shadow of white death had passed. While this is passing, a new element comes into imaginative literature; and we find it to be essentially due to the deferred influence of Platonism. In the beautiful myth of Psyche, we can see it prefigured.

By the ancients Plato was of course admired, just as he is by the moderns, not only as a philosopher but as a supreme literary artist. In antiquity, however, no deep-going influence from him on imaginative literature, or on the modes of feeling expressed in it, had yet begun. His doctrines continued to be expounded by Academic teachers, and at last found a new and more elaborate systematic expression; but this came too late for effect on literature or art of any kind in the ancient world. It was, however, in various remarkable ways preserved and transmitted through the succeeding ages, and thus came to permeate the new culture that arose after the dissolution of the old. A thought arrived at by Graeco-Roman civilisation only at the end was thus present to the new civilisation of the West from its beginning. Among other things, there appeared in the world, after a long and complex transition, the elements of a new kind of love; something not without sex, yet directed in a new way to the inward essence of the individual. In this kind of love there is a metaphysical element; to be seen, under its various modes, in Dante, in Shakespeare, in Shelley, in Leopardi. Of course it is not to be found in all modern literature; but, as a distinctive thing in poetry, this metaphysical element, which communicates a new excitement to the emotion of love, seems to appear first in the late Middle Ages, and to arrive at an expression not yet exhausted in modern times. It may apparently die out for a season and give place to the rendering simply of beautiful form, or even to the abandonment of beauty for "reality" in a sense opposite to Plato's; but it is one of the things that we may be confident will not perish any more than poetry or art itself.

This is the new thing that is prefigured in the myth of Cupid and Psyche. Allegory is of course not alien to the *Metamorphoses*. That the whole story is in a general way an allegory of an individual human life is made plain at the end. The change of Lucius into the shape of an ass and his return to human shape signifies, on Platonic principles, the descent of the soul into the flux of sense and its recovery of its own nature. This is indicated by the detail that Lucius receives back his "servant Candidus," in other words, his white horse. It is by this horse, which means the nobler emotions, that the charioteer, that is, the intellectual part of the soul, is aided in keeping the upward path. Here, however, there is only a quite obvious allegory. The last book of the *Metamorphoses* is simply an expression of the ideal of an ascetic discipline predominant in ethics at the end of the ancient world. This was not a new thing, but only a form of something very old; the selected life of philosophy or religion remote from the crowd. The new thing was expressed in a more spontaneous and less conscious way.

Having first read the story of Cupid and Psyche in Pater's *Marius the Epicurean*, I did not in his rendering, beautiful as it is, perceive the allegory that came into my mind on reading it in Apuleius himself. In fact, this allegory is incompatible with Pater's implied thesis, that in the second century the ancient world, so far as its resources were within itself, was dead; that nothing was left but a frozen beauty; that a renewal of inward and spiritual life could only come from without. This would undoubtedly be true if the official Stoicism had been the final and adequate expression of all that was best in classical antiquity. Pater's diagnosis of the outworn, though noble, creed that reigned with Marcus Aurelius is admirable. The sceptical reflections of Marius on its inadequacy might very well have been those of a refined and contemplative spirit in the period itself. Ancient civilisation, however, had longer to live and a subtler doctrine to bring forth. The ultimate renewal of its inner life was to come from deeper metaphysics; and the spring of this was in the Hellenic past. And when ancient thought and feeling, after its long postponed but inevitable period of latency, came to life again, the new quickening element that made of it something different from the old was a metaphysical doctrine going beyond the Stoic and Epicurean naturalism. The formula of return to nature and to antiquity, by which Pater, in his historical studies of the Renaissance, had tried to sum up the new movement, he evidently felt afterwards to be insufficient; but, though a thinker as well as an artist, he was never much drawn to metaphysics. Hence, in returning for himself to antiquity by the way of historical romance, he failed to discover within the ancient civilisation the really existent causes of renewed vitality. Mixing legend with history, he sought in the Christian Church of the second century the promise of a new dawn; whereas, in truth, it was the metaphysics of the following three centuries that made the Church in some respects a transmitter of deeper insight. This deeper insight, at length restored in its native form when the time came for the winter sleep to go, made the new dawn, amid all the vigorous secular and artistic interests of renascent Europe, not a mere cyclical "return of the pagan world."

What returns to life is, in fine, Psyche, the soul become a new goddess. That is the first and indisputable point of her story in Apuleius. When seen, she is found to be more beautiful than Venus; so that the devotees of Venus turn from their goddess and worship the mortal maiden, Psyche. This, then, is the new kind of love that is coming into the world, the love of the soul. The ancient goddess grows jealous and angry, and stirs up her son Cupid to avenge her by making Psyche fall in love with some low object. Instead of this, having beheld her he falls in love with Psyche himself, and places her in a terrestrial paradise; where, however, she is warned against trying to see him in his proper shape. Here, as in all such stories, there comes the Orphic fall. The jealousy of her sisters—themselves beautiful, but not beyond ordinary beauty—arouses her animosity; though not successfully till they have persuaded her that the god of Love is really a venomous serpent who means to devour her and her offspring. She therefore seeks to destroy Love, but he is revealed as divine, and her love becomes more impassioned. She does not escape, however, from the consequences of her fault. A drop of oil from the lamp she has carried to view him wounds the god, and he flies away to his mother's house to be healed; leaving Psyche to wander through the world under the eyes of the angry Venus—"magnae Veneris inevitabiles oculos." Ceres and Juno, to whom she appeals, refuse to help her; unwillingly, but they dare not offend Venus. In their place, voices from nature tell her how to perform the tasks set by the terrible goddess.

Till we come to these tasks, we seem to read, without express interpretation, the story of the end of the ancient world, the quarrel between flesh and spirit. At the last, we catch a glimpse of hope that the new will be something better and not worse. Let us imagine ourselves with Psyche cast out into the wilderness: then the stages of the return can be interpreted by knowledge of the centuries that were for Apuleius in the future but are for us in the past. Psyche's task of sorting various kinds of seeds confusedly mixed, which is performed for her by ants, points evidently, though not so evidently that it does not need saying, to the logic-chopping of the schoolmen, under whose reign the modern languages of Europe took on their differences from those of antiquity[1]. Her next task is to gather the gold-coloured

[1] By a curious coincidence, a little work of Peripatetic logic attributed to Apuleius, but not by him, comes very early in this process.

wool from the fleeces of certain sheep. These, however, she is told, are savage, and cannot be approached during the heat of the day without danger. She must wait till the afternoon when their rage has abated, and then gather the wool that they have left on the bushes. Here we may find beneath the symbolism the plundering raids and wars of the barbarians. A new poetry has the task imposed upon it of rendering them in song and story; but it must wait till the fierce action of the new "heroic age" has ceased and can be made simply an object of contemplation. Next, Psyche is required to bring to Venus a portion of the waters of Styx. This means that the new Muse must go as deep and as far as Dante from the light of heaven, so that the new beauty into which metaphysical thought has entered may emerge at the end. Finally, she is commanded to go to the house of Orcus and bring to Venus some of the beauty of Proserpine to renew her own. This also, with help as always from friendly guides, she does successfully; but she almost loses everything at last through the ineradicable curiosity native to the soul. Having obeyed every prohibition so far, and returned safely, she cannot refrain from opening the box in which the gift is enclosed, so that, to please her lover when he comes, she may take some of the beauty it contains. She sees nothing, but falls into a sleep like death. Cupid, having now recovered from his wound, arrives just in time, wipes from her face the sleep, puts it again into the box, and tells her to take it to his mother. Here too there is a clear meaning in the allegory. The beauty of Proserpine, by which Venus and Psyche, the more ancient and the newer goddess, are alike refreshed, is the beauty drawn from sleep. Before the renovated world, with its changed quality of emotion, could emerge, there had to be a break in culture. And the aid given to Psyche all through seems to mean that only by some providential destiny could the human soul come to a term of the apparently fruitless wanderings of the middle period. The outcome of the history is declared when it is said that Psyche "longe vegetior ab inferis recurrit[1]." After the end of all wanderings, the marriage of Cupid and Psyche, by the determination of the gods, is to be eternal; and their offspring is "Voluptas." The joy of life—"Youth and Joy," as Milton expresses it—is born again; and the metaphysical philosophy of the Platonists, instead of finding its ultimate expression in retreat from the world, transfigures the world and takes up sense into spirit.

By another coincidence beyond those mentioned, there is a singular dialogue going under the name of Apuleius which contains a most audacious prediction of the downfall in some long distant future of the religion that has turned from light to darkness and from life to death and condemned the visible world as a place to flee from. The reason why the anonymous dialogue of *Asclepius* was ascribed to Apuleius is evident. He mentions in different places of his writings[2] compositions

[1] Cf. Pater, *Studies in the History of the Renaissance*, 1st ed. p. 200: "And now it was seen that the mediaeval spirit too had done something for the destiny of the antique. By hastening the decline of art, by withdrawing interest from it, and yet keeping the thread of its traditions, it had suffered the human mind to repose, that it might awake when day came, with eyes refreshed, to those antique forms." But this, though true, is incomplete. It would explain the Hellenism of Landor, but not of Shelley; the return of concrete beauty at the Renaissance, but not beauty that is half-metaphysical.

[2] See *Apology*, c. 55 and *Florida*, c. 18.

written by him in honour of Aesculapius. What he says of them does not at all correspond to the contents of the *Asclepius*, but it explains the ascription. This dialogue is held to be a compilation from various sources: the passage referred to is probably the latest and cannot be earlier than about the end of the fourth century. The whole belongs to what is called the Hermetic literature. Its manner is that of prophecy, not of logical method, and there is no sign of any influence from Neo-Platonism. Some of its obscurity is no doubt due to unskilful translation from the Greek. In substance, however, it sets forth a philosophical religion, Hellenic in spirit, which is called "the religion of the mind." A lamentation over Egypt appears to be symbolical: its ruin is that of the old religion and civilisation. The teaching has elements that appealed to the Renaissance more distinctively than they can have done to the Platonising contemporaries of the writer. Bruno took it over with enthusiastic sympathy; for it includes a whole-hearted pantheistic defence of visible beauty and of the joy in all forms of life. The oracular Hermes or Thoth, declaring that nature creates by a kind of imagination[1], glorifies the world and man; makes man in this respect superior to the gods, that he has two sources, the intellectual and the animal or sensitive[2]; affirms that divinity, if terms of sex are applied to it, must be called bisexual, and deifies both male and female in man[3]. No higher place is reserved for the ascetic life. Man is expressly celebrated as making the gods in his own image when he imposes his ideal of beautiful form on statues. "Gods arose alive on earth from under stroke

[1] c. 3: "natura per species imaginans mundum."

[2] c. 9. [3] cc. 20–21.

of human hands," is already a thought to exult in. That only devotion of the mind, without animal sacrifice, is to be offered to the supreme deity, all else being a desecration[1], is, of course, a point common to all the philosophical religion of the time, pagan or Christian.

A work quite different from this in literary form, but having something in common with it that may be easily recognised, is the poem of Rutilius Namatianus, *De Reditu Suo*. To the journey which he describes, his "home-coming from Rome to Gaul," the date assigned is 416. The poem is a lively and agreeable narrative of travel, and republications of it have been frequent[2]. It is generally agreed that the outbursts, remarkable for their vigour and incisiveness, against the Jews and the monks, are really directed against Christianity. Though his French editor denies this, we cannot have any serious doubt what is meant when Judaism is called the *radix stultitiae*. Passing Capraria, an abode of monks, the traveller exclaims, "Squalet lucifugis insula plena viris." Then later, Rutilius describes a young man, who may have been a personal friend, as having sacrificed all the gifts of fortune and left his wife and family and every human association, to go into a living grave.

[1] c. 41.

[2] There is a recent elaborate French and a rather less elaborate English edition, each with introduction, notes and translation; the English translation in verse and the French in prose.

Rutilii Claudii Namatiani De Reditu Suo Libri Duo. The Home-coming of Rutilius Namatianus from Rome to Gaul in the Year 416 A.D. Edited by Charles Harries Keene, and translated by George F. Savage-Armstrong. London, 1907.

Cl. Rutilius Namatianus. Édition Critique, accompagnée d'une Traduction française et d'un Index, &c. Par J. Vessereau. Paris, 1904.

Infelix putat illuvie caelestia pasci,
Seque premit laesis saevior ipse deis.
Non, rogo, deterior Circeis secta venenis?
Tunc mutabantur corpora, nunc animi[1].

He himself, a Gaul by birth, had gained distinction as a Roman official, and he has no sympathy with the men of rank in his own age who

hurried, torn with inward strife,
The wilderness to find.

To him they seemed to be deserting every attempt to be of use in the world out of shrinking from the risks of life and fear of offended gods.

With Rutilius and with the author of the *Asclepius*, Gaston Boissier[2] brings into association Macrobius, who, like Rutilius, was a Roman official; being described at the head of each of his works as "Ambrosius Theodosius Macrobius, vir clarissimus et illustris." He too, as he tells us, was not of Roman birth[3]. He seems, from what he says, to have been born in the Greek-speaking part of the Empire. Though he nowhere introduces the slightest allusion to Christianity, he was undoubtedly a member of the pagan party in his time. The personages of his dialogues are its chiefs at Rome, Praetextatus and Symmachus and their friends; to whom, in the opinion of an expert on the subject, we largely owe the preservation of culture in Western Europe[4]. It is interesting to

[1] *De Reditu Suo*, I. 523–6.

[2] *La Fin du Paganisme*. 2 vols. Paris, 1891.

[3] *Saturnalia*, Praef., 11–12.

[4] See a short notice by Mr F. W. Hall in the *Classical Review*, February–March, 1922, p. 32: "What has preserved the Latin classics for us is not the Roman libraries, but the efforts of the pagan nobles of the Theodosian epoch—the 'anti-Christian Fronde,' as they have been called. These men kept alive the ancient

trace their descendants, by notes in Gibbon, among members of the senatorial families. Their posterity in the sixth century of course were Christians, real or nominal. The great-great-grandson of the pagan Symmachus was the father-in-law of Boethius, who belonged to the family of the Anicii, which had been Christian from an early period. Boethius and his father-in-law were both executed under Theodoric the Ostrogoth on a charge of conspiracy to restore the powers of the Senate; and, soon after, the Senate itself disappeared. In the meantime, while the old structure of life was crumbling, the preservation of learning had been secured by a tacit compromise. The complete reticence of Macrobius on all questions disputed between pagans and Christians permitted him to become one of the most authorised instructors of the Christian age.

This position was not obtained without merits of his own. Gibbon has said in a well-known passage: "The senator Boethius is the last of the Romans whom Cato or Tully could have acknowledged for their countryman[1]." Macrobius, though earlier, has not been so successful in writing a piece of literature that can be read with pleasure simply as such and apart from the desire for acquaintance with the kind of thought and knowledge that existed in his time; but, if justice is done to

learning long enough for the Christian Church to recover its senses and breed up men of the type of Cassiodorus in the place of the early fanatics." In his *Companion to Classical Texts* (Oxford, 1913), p. 65, the same author says: "Q. Aurelius Symmachus, famous as an orator, administrator and man of letters, is also famous as the champion of paganism whose protest in 384 against the abolition of the altar of Victory is perhaps the noblest defence of a dying creed that has ever been made."

[1] *Decline and Fall of the Roman Empire*, ch. XXXIX, ed. Bury, vol. IV. pp. 197–8.

him, it will be acknowledged that, while he frankly describes his own works as compilations written for the instruction of his son, they are more than mere compilations; for they do in fact set forth an organic body of science and criticism, and a distinctive philosophical doctrine. It is agreeable to know that Boethius, writing more than a century later, commended his treatises[1], and thus probably did something to give them their vogue.

The doctrine of Macrobius and of Boethius was essentially the same, though Macrobius was a pagan and Boethius perhaps compiled some text-books of Christian theology[2]. In his philosophical work, Boethius is as silent as Macrobius about Christianity: the difference is that in him the antiquarian interest shown by Macrobius in the ancient cult has disappeared. The philosophy in both of them is a simplified Neo-Platonism adapted to the Latin West. They were exceedingly successful in conveying it to the Middle Ages along with the elements of ancient science, mathematical and astronomical. My object being to write a literary study of Macrobius himself, I do not propose either to discuss this influence in detail or to go into the investigation of the ancient sources of his criticism and philosophy further than is absolutely necessary[3]. It must be said that the Middle Ages were more equitable to him than

[1] In the Commentary on the *Isagoge* of Porphyry: see Schedler, *Die Philosophie des Macrobius*, &c., p. 104, n. 2.

[2] The genuineness of these is still doubtful.

[3] The following works have been consulted:

L. Petit, *De Macrobio Ciceronis Interprete Philosopho*. Paris, 1866.

Hugo Linke, *Quaestiones de Macrobii Saturnaliorum Fontibus*. Breslau, 1880.

G. Wissowa, *De Macrobii Saturnaliorum Fontibus*. Breslau, 1880.

M. Schedler, *Die Philosophie des Macrobius und ihr Einfluss auf*

the modern time has yet shown itself. From the preface to an early printed edition (Venice, 1528), it appears that some scholars of the Renaissance would have nothing to do with him because he dared to find faults in Virgil and to use words not in Cicero. In more recent times, he has been condemned as a pedant because, instead of simply discussing the poet's words, he treats him sometimes as an authority on religious ritual or on the science of his age. There is no doubt occasionally a touch of the excessive deference to authority that came with expiring antiquity; but, on the whole, Macrobius proves himself not only a man of great culture in the sense of knowing the best that has been thought and said in the world, but a man of sound and independent judgment. What was the nature of the literary, scientific and philosophical tradition which he handed down, I shall try to make clear by a fairly circumstantial exposition and discussion of his two extant works.

die Wissenschaft des christlichen Mittelalters. Münster i. W., 1916.

Œuvres de Macrobe. Traduction nouvelle par MM. Henri Descamps, N. A. Dubois, Laass d'Aguen, A. Ubicini Martelli. 3 vols. Paris, 1845–7. [Latin and French, with introductions and notes.]

For Macrobius, I have of course used the text of Eyssenhardt (2nd ed., Leipzig, 1893).

II

THE SATURNALIA

IN a dedication of the *Saturnalia* to his son Eustachius, the author states his purpose with a candour that ought to have disarmed fault-finders. The composition is to be a medley taken from writers of all ages, Greek and Latin. The very words of the ancient authors will sometimes be carried over, yet a certain new quality will be given to them because they have been, as it were, digested and assimilated by one mind. Nothing could be more fairly said; and he is equally candid in telling us of the licence he has taken in bringing together the friends who are supposed to meet at the house of Vettius Praetextatus on the occasion of the Saturnalia. In this licence, he claims to follow Plato; who, he says, made Parmenides and Socrates discuss abstruse subjects together, though Socrates can scarcely have reached boyhood when Parmenides was an old man[1]. Therefore he will leave the age of the persons at the time of the dialogue a little vague. In reality, some were too young to have met Praetextatus as grown men.

For general understanding, it will suffice to say that the chiefs of the Roman nobility, with some unofficial scholars[2], meet on the Saturnalia at the house of

[1] i. 1, 5: "quippe Socrate ita Parmenides antiquior, ut huius pueritia vix illius adprehenderit senectutem, et tamen inter illos de rebus arduis disputatur." Of course the authority of Macrobius is not conclusive on the point of chronology; but we see that it was not the tradition of antiquity that Plato was a literally exact reporter.

[2] i. 1, 1: "Romanae nobilitatis proceres doctique alii."

Praetextatus for discussion of liberal studies. They are interested in details of old cults, in the theory of religion, in comparisons between the Greek and Latin poets, especially of Virgil with Homer, in old stories and in old usages as compared with the present. Above all other studies is placed philosophy[1]; but Macrobius has reserved more express discussion of philosophical questions for his Commentary on the *Somnium Scipionis.*

A beginning is made with a disputation on the mode of reckoning the day, grammatical usages as illustrated by Ennius, and similar topics. The interlocutors are interested precisely in the questions that Seneca treated as examples of idle antiquarianism[2]; but pedantic use of old expressions is discountenanced. Let us live modestly like the ancients, says Avienus[3], but speak the language of our own day. This may seem to imply a conventionally idyllic view of the past; but we shall see later that Macrobius assigns to his spokesmen a penetrating refutation of what it was customary (as it always is) to say about the simplicity of old times compared with present luxury. The permission of occasional intoxication which Seneca appears to give[4] might have furnished them with a contrast to their own more sober manners. But, in substance, they agree with the more liberal passages of Seneca in which he assigns a place

[1] i. 24, 21.

[2] *Ad Paulinum de Brevitate Vitae,* 13, 5.

[3] i. 5, 2.

[4] *Ad Serenum de Tranquillitate Animi*, 17, 9: "Solonem Arcesilamque indulsisse vino credunt, Catoni ebrietas obiecta est: facilius efficiet, quisquis obiecit ei, crimen honestum quam turpem Catonem." According to Plato, Seneca adds, the height of poetic inspiration cannot be reached with a sober mind; and according to Aristotle there is no great wit without a mixture of madness. In short, to reach greatness of expression, the mind must let itself go (17, 11). No doubt the experience of the tragedian suggested something to the philosopher.

for disinterested curiosity and recognises pleasure among the things to be sought in life. The grave ancients would have had no quarrel with the conclusion of Milton:

> He who of those delights can judge, and spare
> To interpose them oft, is not unwise.

No implied apology, however, is needed, as regards gravity of subject or treatment, for the *Saturnalia* of Macrobius. The setting of the banquet, with the form of dialogue, gives a certain amenity, and enables the author to pass easily from topic to topic without too much logical arrangement; but he sometimes forgets the conversational form, and definitely refers the reader to some author, as if he were writing a treatise[1]. The most interesting part of Book i is, in fact, a rather elaborate treatise on the solar or cosmic theory of the origins of religion.

This is put into the mouth of Praetextatus, who is recognised by all as the great authority on questions about ancient religion. The starting-point is the search for the origin of the Saturnalia; that feast being the occasion of the meeting. First, Praetextatus reserves his personal view of religion itself. He will discuss the Saturnalia not in relation to the secret nature of the divinity, but only in relation to the fables and the physical explanations given of them[2]. It is perhaps not too much to say that what he proposes is to offer a science of the rites and myths uncomplicated by questions of philosophical edification.

For the general theory set forth, there were sources about which a few words must be said. The principal

[1] See, for example, the note for the benefit of the "diligens lector" in bk i. 16, 30.

[2] i. 7, 18.

source was thought to have been indicated by some coincidences with the Oration of Julian on the Sun-god. Julian himself tells us that his source was Iamblichus[1]. Hence Wissowa[2] came to the conclusion that Julian and Macrobius alike depend on a lost work of Iamblichus περὶ θεῶν, but that Macrobius did not simply take over this, but had other sources; for much of his matter is Roman, not Greek. Schedler, writing later, regards it as now proved that the common source was a lost work of Porphyry "On the Sun"[3]. The two commentators agree in placing hypothetical Latin books between Macrobius and his Greek source, whether Porphyry or Iamblichus, not only for this portion of his work but for others. Why this should be necessary, I am unable to see. Macrobius knew Greek perhaps better than Latin, and refers to Plotinus and Porphyry in a way that shows real knowledge of them. But no doubt he used Roman antiquarian writers for his facts; and it is not likely that he could find the facts presented anywhere clear of theory. What it is now necessary to insist on is that Macrobius was himself an intelligent writer, and not simply a passive recipient of the intelligence of predecessors. In any case, there is no prospect of an end to the search for sources. Porphyry compiled before Iamblichus[4], Iamblichus before Julian, and Julian before

[1] Or. IV. 146 A, 150 D (παρ' οὗ καὶ τἆλλα πάντα ἐκ πολλῶν μικρὰ ἐλάβομεν). Cf. 157 D.

[2] *De Macrobii Saturnaliorum Fontibus*, p. 41.

[3] *Die Philosophie des Macrobius*, &c., p. 98: "Die Quelle für diese Deutungskunst bietet, wie die neuere Forschung ermittelt hat, die Schrift des Porphyr über den Helios, nicht, wie Wissowa nachgewiesen zu haben glaubte, das Werk περὶ θεῶν des Jamblich."

[4] For the *De Antro Nympharum*, he himself cites Cronius as a source; and Cronius may have depended on Numenius, who is also cited.

Macrobius; and all that we know as a datum is that Macrobius and Julian certainly had a common source, and that Julian's direct source was Iamblichus, whom Macrobius nowhere mentions.

The beginnings of the solar theory of religion do not seem to be traceable, like the "Euhemerist" theory that the gods are deified men, to a particular name. We may be content to give Macrobius credit for a very circumstantial and coherent statement of it. He leads up to the examination of mythology by a preliminary discussion of ritual. The rites of the Saturnalia are declared to be older than the foundation of Rome. At first they included human sacrifices, said to have been commanded by oracles. The oracles were at length evaded by skilful interpretation, and the sacrifices commuted into harmless offerings of effigies or of parts of vegetables. Two of the stories may be quoted. Hercules, it is related, returning through Italy with the oxen of Geryon, got the sacrifices commuted by a new interpretation of the Greek (καὶ κεφαλὰς Ἅιδῃ καὶ τῷ πατρὶ πέμπετε φῶτα) into an offering of effigies in human form and lighted candles (quia non solum virum sed et lumina φῶτα significat)[1]. Albinus Caecina adds the story that a sacrifice of children to the goddess Mania, the Mother of the Lares, was restored by Tarquinius Superbus at the Compitalia in accordance with an oracle of Apollo, and that the Consul Junius Brutus, after the expulsion of Tarquin, substituted heads of garlic and poppies by reinterpreting the "capita" mentioned in the oracle[2].

On this subject of commutations there was abundance of antiquarian lore, as may be seen also in Porphyry *De Abstinentia*, where all blood-sacrifice is treated as

[1] i. 7, 31. [2] i. 7, 34–35.

something unholy. This was the normal view of philosophers in the period, as is indicated in a speech of Horus (another interlocutor in the dialogues) when he claims on behalf of the old Egyptian religion the exclusion of all such rites—a view which, it is to be feared, is not confirmed by modern Egyptologists. The Egyptians, Horus says, did not receive Saturn or Serapis at all before the death of Alexander, and even under the Ptolemies would not admit their temples within the walls of any town, because their rites were polluted with the blood of beasts[1]. Unfortunately, this was only a "counsel of perfection." Julian and his friend Sallust, themselves Neo-Platonic philosophers, when they restored the old as against the newly-established religion, had to defend animal sacrifices as part of the total system. We may be surprised, on reading Julian's confession of disappointment at the indifference to the restored cult in the towns, that the sacrificial customs should not simply have been allowed to lapse; but we know historically that, years later, the Christian Church could only suppress the custom of sacrificing in the country districts by a severe persecution. There was no pagan popular religion apart from it. And of course the Church carried on by symbolism the idea of blood-sacrifice in its own cult. Yet Heraclitus, five centuries before the Christian era, had struck at the root of the whole doctrine of cleansing by blood. So slow is progress, and so much is it an affair of compromise.

As we go on, we meet with other "counsels of perfection." All are glad that the old barbaric ritual is gone;

[1] i. 7, 15: "nam quia numquam fas fuit Aegyptiis pecudibus aut sanguine sed precibus et ture solo placare deos, his autem duobus advenis hostiae erant ex more mactandae, fana eorum extra pomerium locaverunt."

but, at the same time, general consent recognises in the primeval order of society an innocence that has been lost. In the reign of Saturn, there was no distinction of freedom and slavery[1], and all wealth was held in common[2]. An expression of contempt for slaves is put into the mouth of Euangelus, whom all the rest agree from the first in regarding as a disagreeable person, to be received only out of politeness; while Praetextatus, the ideal pagan noble, completely takes over the view of Seneca[3] in arguing for the equal humanity of slaves, whose condition is due to fortune and not to difference of nature. Jupiter himself, according to an old story, had reproved the cruelty of a Roman master to a slave[4]. Illustrations are given—preferably from the early times of the Republic—of religious ceremonies in which, according to the antiquaries, the virtues of slaves, both men and women, were commemorated.

After the preliminaries on ritual, we proceed to mythology. There is cursory mention of the opinions of some that Janus was a king who was deified for introducing religious rites[5], and that Saturn and his wife Ops were discoverers of the fruits of the ground[6]; but all the systematic theorising is in terms of solar explanations. More exactly, perhaps, the theory ought to be called cosmic. The sun stands for the whole as being visibly predominant, so that the powers of the universe may be treated as his aspects; but the idea of correlation also is used. Saturn and Ops, we are told, are, according to some, Heaven and Earth[7]. Serapis and Isis

[1] i. 7, 26. [2] i. 8, 4.

[3] Macrobius does not refer to Seneca, the Stoic philosophy as a system being out of date; but there are clear traces of the use of his writings.

[4] i. 11, 3–4. [5] i. 9, 2–4. [6] i. 10, 19. [7] i. 10, 20.

are interpreted as Sun and Earth or the receptive nature of things[1].

The method of proof is by identifications, ritual or traditional or etymological, of deities with one another, ending in identification with some deity unquestionably solar. The name of Janus associates him with Diana and so with Apollo, admittedly a solar god[2]. He may also be treated as directly signifying the cosmic revolution[3]. He is sometimes represented with four faces ("a double Janus") as looking to the four quarters of the world and including all in his divinity[4]. The explanation cited from the augur M. Messala, that he joined together the four elements, consisting of two groups, the heavy and the light, in one whole[5], is obviously a fanciful accommodation to Greek philosophy.

The discussion about the gradual formation of the Calendar, with its dedications of months to gods (as January to Janus), we may pass over lightly. It is interesting, however, to learn with what care for the susceptibilities of conservative religion Julius Caesar carried through his reforms[6]. Another point that may just be mentioned is the casuistry, cited from the Roman law, about works permissible on days of rest. The head of a household was allowed to employ labourers to set free an ox that had fallen into a pit; and, if a broken beam of a roof threatened to fall, it might lawfully be propped up[7].

The return being made from digressions to the centre of the argument, Praetextatus claims the right to draw

[1] i. 20, 18: "Isis iuncta religione celebratur, quae est vel terra vel natura rerum subiacens soli."

[2] i. 9, 5–10. [3] i. 9, 11. [4] i. 9, 13.

[5] i. 9, 14: "copulavit circumdato caelo."

[6] i. 14, 6–12. [7] i. 16, 11.

largely from the poets. It is not, he says, by vain superstition, but by divine reason, that they refer almost all the gods, "at least those that are under the heaven," to the sun[1]. The reservation here must not be neglected as something casual or merely formal. The religion of the philosophers themselves was not solar or cosmic, but was more metaphysical, more "transcendent." The popular polytheism, from their point of view, symbolised a pantheism which was part but not the whole of what they regarded as philosophic truth. It is with this part, however, that they are now occupied. The various powers of the sun, says Praetextatus, gave names to gods: "unde ἓν τὸ πᾶν sapientum principes prodiderunt[2]."

In a manner suggested by the Heraclitean philosophy, the opposite effects ascribed to each deity are explained by the opposite effects of the sun. Neptune is at once the Earth-shaker and the Securer[3]. Mercury both awakens and sends to sleep the minds or eyes of men[4]. Apollo is the Saviour and also sends pestilence; and yet again, the pestilence is sent in championship of the good[5].

The source of these explanations, we may see by the names of the philosophic authorities cited, is Stoic; and the Heracliteanism of the Stoics is no doubt responsible for many etymologies in the manner of the *Cratylus*[6].

[1] i. 17, 2. [2] i. 17, 4.

[3] i. 17, 22: "ut Neptunum, quem alias Ἐνοσίχθονα, id est terram moventem, alias Ἀσφαλίωνα, id est stabilientem, vocant."

[4] *Il.* xxiv. 343 is quoted.

[5] i. 17, 23. This is, of course, an allusion to the opening of the *Iliad*. In the theory of mythology, we observe that the Greek stories are simply carried over, just as in the Latin poets.

[6] *E.g.* i. 17, 35: "Camerienses, qui sacram soli incolunt insulam Ἀειγενέτῃ Apollini immolant τῷ τὸν ἥλιον ἀεὶ γίγνεσθαι καὶ ἀεὶ γεννᾶν, id est quod semper exoriens gignitur, quodque ipse generat universa inseminando fovendo producendo alendo augendoque."

Their doctrine that the universe is one community accounts for some distinctive explanations. The idea of a national god is repudiated. Apollo, we are told, is called Πατρῷος not as worshipped according to the religion of a particular race or State, but because the sun is the generating cause of all things; whence the Romans also call Janus the Father, celebrating the sun under that name[1]. He is called the shepherd or herdsman not from the fable about his service with Admetus, but because the sun pastures all that the earth brings forth[2].

Apollo and Liber Pater are the same[3]; but more directly it may be proved that Liber Pater, that is, Dionysus, is the sun. The proof is that in a secret religious observance the sun in the upper hemisphere is called Apollo, in the lower or nocturnal hemisphere Dionysus[4]. Also Dionysus is represented as of various ages according to the season of the year. Those differences of age refer to the sun. Thus the Egyptians at the winter solstice bring the god from the shrine on a certain day as an infant; at the spring equinox, they present him under the form of a young man; at the summer solstice, he is figured with a beard; and in his fourth form as descending to old age[5]. In an oracle of Apollo Clarius, the same god, Liber, is called Ἰαώ, interpreted generally as the highest god, and specially as the autumnal sun[6]. In Orphic verses also, Liber and the

[1] i. 17, 42.

[2] i. 17, 43; cf. 45: "quapropter universi pecoris antistes et vere pastor agnoscitur."

[3] i. 18, 1–6. [4] i. 18, 8. [5] i. 18, 10.

[6] i. 18, 19–20. The lines suggest a gnostic attempt to bring Judaism into the general synthesis; but Macrobius does not seem to know anything of this. We may suspect composite authorship;

sun are shown to be one and the same by the astronomical imagery in the dress of Dionysus[1].

Mars and Liber are joined by many in such a way as to show that they are one god. Hence Bacchus is called Ἐνυάλιος, which is one of the proper names of Mars[2]. In the wreathing of the point of the thyrsus (replaced among the Lacedaemonians by a spear) with ivy, there is a moral meaning. It indicates that the impulse to war should be repressed[3]. Being identical with one another, Bacchus (or Liber) and Mars are also identical with the sun[4]. Mercury and Apollo too are the same. The sun's movement between the upper and the lower hemispheres is signified by the representation of Mercury in fable as the messenger between the celestial and infernal gods[5]. He is not called Argiphontes because he slew Argus; but under the form of the fable, Argus stands for the sky distinct with stars, which is as it were slain when the sun blots them from the sight of mortals by day[6].

One fanciful explanation cited from the physical philosophers is that Dionysus is Διὸς νοῦς[7]. An inter-

some theological "liberal" correcting the exclusiveness of a Jewish "Sibylline oracle."

> *φράζεο τὸν πάντων ὕπατον θεὸν ἔμμεν Ἰαώ,*
> *χείματι μέν τ' Ἀίδην, Δία δ' εἴαρος ἀρχομένοιο,*
> *Ἠέλιον δὲ θέρευς, μετοπώρου δ' ἁβρὸν Ἰαώ.*

[1] i. 18, 22. [2] i. 19, 1–2.

[3] i. 19, 2: "sed cum thyrsum tenet, quid aliud quam latens telum gerit, cuius mucro hedera lambente protegitur? quod ostendit vinculo quodam patientiae obligandos impetus belli. habet enim hedera vinciendi obligandique naturam."

[4] i. 19, 4; cf. 6. Both are fiery gods; "et certe ratio naturalis exigit, ut di caloris caelestis parentes magis nominibus quam re substantiaque divisi sint." [5] i. 19, 10–11. [6] i. 19, 12–13.

[7] i. 18, 15: "physici Διόνυσον Διὸς νοῦν, quia solem mundi mentem esse dixerunt. mundus autem vocatur caelum, quod appellant Iovem."

pretation that comes from Plotinus, though Macrobius does not here refer to him, is that the sexual attribute of Hermes symbolises the eternally creative activity of νοῦς in the cosmos[1]. It is interesting to notice this continuity of feeling with the early worship of natural powers. However ascetic the Neo-Platonists might be personally; however, in their theoretical philosophy, they might place the stability of the life of intellect above the flux of birth; they were careful not to blaspheme sex. For it was part of their view that the world-process must always go on. Thus Julian, whose personal chastity is denied by no one, takes occasion to glorify Aphrodite as sharing in productive power with the Sun[2]. And Porphyry gives as one reason for his nominal marriage[3] when declining to old age[4], the purpose of conciliating the gods of birth (τοὺς γενεθλίους θεούς), as Socrates wrote verses before his death to propitiate the more popular Muses in case his philosophising was not accepted by them as a sufficient service[5].

There is a point of contact with Julian when we are told that one proof of the identity of Aesculapius with Apollo is that he is believed to have been born of him[6]. Hercules is "that power of the sun which endows the

[1] i. 19, 14.

[2] Or. IV. 150 C: Ἀφροδίτη δὲ αὐτῷ συναίτιος, ἡ θέλγουσα μὲν τὰς ψυχὰς ἡμῶν σὺν εὐφροσύνῃ, καταπέμπουσα δὲ εἰς γῆν ἐξ αἰθέρος αὐγὰς ἡδίστας καὶ ἀκηράτους αὐτοῦ τοῦ χρυσίου στιλπνοτέρας.

[3] *Ad Marcellam*, c. 33.

[4] *Ibid.* c. 1.

[5] *Ibid.* c. 2: οὑτωσὶ γὰρ καὶ αὐτὸς ἀπομειλιττόμενος τοὺς ἐν τῇ κωμῳδοτραγῳδίᾳ προστάτας δαίμονας τὸν γαμικὸν ὕμνον ἀγωνίσασθαι οὐκ ὤκνησα.

[6] i. 20, 4: "quod ex illo natus creditur." Cf. Julian, Or. IV. 144 B. Apollo Musegetes begets in the world Asclepius, whom he has with him also before the world: γεννᾷ μὲν ἐν κόσμῳ τὸν Ἀσκληπιόν, ἔχει δὲ αὐτὸν καὶ πρὸ τοῦ κόσμου παρ' ἑαυτῷ.

human race with virtue by which it imitates the gods[1]." A similar interpretation of Minerva is cited from Porphyry. Since the goddess conveys prudence or foreknowledge to human minds, she is rightly described as springing from the head of the chief god, that is, from the highest part of the ether, whence the sun takes his origin[2].

The death of Adonis, the lamentation of Venus over him, and his return to life, of course Macrobius has no difficulty in explaining on his principles. The solar explanation adopted has become perhaps the best-known of all theories about the origin of a myth. As Adonis is wounded by the boar, so the sun receives a wound as it were from the rough season of winter, goes to the hemisphere of the earth symbolised by Proserpine, and then at the spring equinox returns to the hemisphere symbolised by Venus[3]. The myth of the Mother of the Gods and Attis is to be understood in like manner[4], and so also is that of Isis and Osiris[5]; as is shown by the emblems of the cult in each case.

The signs of the Zodiac are all interpreted as part of the solar religion; and perhaps the theory is most

[1] i. 20, 6: "quippe Hercules ea est solis potestas, quae humano generi virtutem ad similitudinem praestat deorum."

[2] i. 17, 70: "sicut et Porphyrius testatur Minervam esse virtutem solis, quae humanis mentibus prudentiam subministrat. nam ideo haec dea Iovis capite prognata memoratur, id est de summa aetheris parte edita, unde origo solis est." Cf. Julian, Or. IV. 149 AB, where a slightly different turn is given to the explanation of Athena Pronoia, *ἣν ὁ μὲν μῦθός φησιν ἐκ τῆς τοῦ Διὸς γενέσθαι κορυφῆς, ἡμεῖς δὲ ὅλην ἐξ ὅλου τοῦ βασιλέως Ἡλίου προβληθῆναι συνεχομένην ἐν αὐτῷ, ταύτῃ διαφέροντες τοῦ μύθου, ὅτι μὴ ἐκ τοῦ ἀκροτάτου μέρους, ὅλην δὲ ἐξ ὅλου.* The poetic myth is here passing over for the philosophers into the idea of "the intellectual sun"; but the Stoic source of the theorising is visible in the notion of fiery or ethereal substance.

[3] i. 21, 1–6. [4] i. 21, 7–10. [5] i. 21, 11–13.

definitely generalised in the explanation of the sign of the Twins. The living of Castor and Pollux by alternate deaths is taken as the symbol of the everlasting alternation between the descent of the sun to the lower regions of the world and the resurrection by which he returns to the summit. Here the sun is not that of Heraclitus, put out and rekindled, as in some of the explanations bearing traces of an earlier cosmology, but is always one and the same[1].

Nemesis, worshipped as against pride, is that one among the manifold powers of the sun of which the nature is to obscure brilliant things and withdraw them from sight, and to make bright and bring to view those that are in the dark[2]. We are reminded here of the old saying, which comes down from the time of the "wise men," that the work of Zeus is to raise up that which was low and to bring down that which was high[3]. Something of the kind we meet with everywhere. In reading, for example, the story of the choice of lots at the end of the *Republic*, especially when every detail is brought out as in the commentary of Proclus, it is difficult to avoid the suggestion that some theosophic saying equivalent to "The last shall be first, and the first last," had long been wandering about the world before it found embodiment in myth or parable.

[1] i. 21, 22: "Gemini autem, qui alternis mortibus vivere creduntur, quid aliud nisi solem unum eundemque significant modo descendentem in ima mundi, modo mundi in summam altitudinem resurgentem?"

[2] i. 22, 1.

[3] Diog. Laert. i. 69 (Chilo): *φασὶ δ' αὐτὸν καὶ Αἰσώπου πυθέσθαι, ὁ Ζεὺς τί εἴη ποιῶν· τὸν δὲ φάναι, 'τὰ μὲν ὑψηλὰ ταπεινῶν, τὰ δὲ ταπεινὰ ὑψῶν.'* Cf. Xen. *Hell.* vi. 4, 23 (Jason of Pherae to the Thebans): *καὶ ὁ θεὸς δέ, ὡς ἔοικε, πολλάκις χαίρει τοὺς μὲν μικροὺς μεγάλους ποιῶν, τοὺς δὲ μεγάλους μικρούς.*

The more penetrating, Praetextatus continues, will find in Pan, who is called Inuus, not the lord of the woodlands, but the sun as ruler of all material substance[1]. This is the real meaning of the name by which the Arcadians worship him (τὸν τῆς ὕλης κύριον). Of this matter, the force of all bodies, whether divine or earthly, forms the essence[2]. His love is Echo, beheld by no eye, but signifying the harmony of the heaven[3].

Finally, it is shown by many stories and figures in the poets, aided by philosophic interpretations, that Jupiter, the king of the gods, is the sun. The gods who, according to Homer and Plato[4], follow him, are the stars. Further proof is found in Assyrian and Egyptian ritual; and the argument is brought to a close with an Orphic invocation in which Zeus is identified at once with Dionysus and with the Sun-god:

ἀγλαὲ Ζεῦ Διόνυσε, πάτερ πόντου, πάτερ αἴης,
Ἥλιε παγγενέτορ πανταίολε χρυσεοφεγγές[5].

All praise the exposition of Praetextatus; but it is not left without critical objection. Euangelus ventures to point out one fault. Virgil has been quoted as meaning the sun and moon when he says "Liber et alma Ceres." But was he not simply imitating some other poet without knowing what the words meant? Or are the Romans, like the Greeks, who raise to the skies everything of their own, to insist on making their poets also philosophers? This leads to a discussion in which the other

[1] i. 22, 2.

[2] i. 22, 3: "cuius materiae vis universorum corporum, seu illa divina sive terrena sint, componit essentiam."

[3] i. 22, 7: "huius Inui amor et deliciae Ἠχώ creditur nullius oculis obnoxia, quod significat harmoniam caeli, quae soli amica est, quasi sphaerarum omnium de quibus nascitur moderatori, nec tamen potest nostris umquam sensibus deprehendi."

[4] i. 23, 4–6. [5] i. 23, 22.

persons of the dialogue undertake to find wisdom and knowledge as well as poetry in Virgil. To Symmachus is assigned the very judicious remark that his glory is neither to be made greater by any one's praises nor lessened by any one's disparagement[1].

Book i ends with a promise of the long and minute examination of Virgilian questions that fills Books iii to vi. Book ii digresses into a collection of witticisms on which there will be something to say; but in the meantime the pause in the argument seems to invite a short discussion of the theory of Macrobius on its merits. For the solar explanation put forward by him is modern as well as ancient, and, after a period of disfavour, may be said again to hold its own in contemporary controversy.

First, we must abstract from that substratum of popular religion which, as modern students of anthropology tell us, the educated Greeks and Romans did not themselves understand from within. Magic, sacrifice and sacrament, so important if we were aiming at an explanation, or even a definition, of religion as a whole, we may leave aside, concentrating attention on the imaginative mythology. If we make this abstraction, then, I think, a fair conclusion will be that Macrobius—proceeding, of course, on the work of predecessors—had successfully determined the real nature of one great normal development of belief.

This development used to be ascribed to "the Aryan race," and it certainly does extend over the whole range of the Aryan-speaking peoples, from the Indians and Persians in the East to the Celts and Teutons in the

[1] i. 24, 8: "haec est quidem, Euangele, Maronis gloria, ut nullius laudibus crescat, nullius vituperatione minuatur."

West and North. Macrobius takes as its typical form that which he knew best, the Greek polytheism, but, as we have seen, not without glances at others; and, in fact, we must add, as he did, to the peoples that took part in this great development, the Babylonians and Egyptians. The curiously twisted local religion of Rome, an affair of ceremonial cult with little mythology, he knew well as an antiquarian, and could make use of his knowledge for the interpretation of Virgil's archaeology; but it contributes to his explanations only by occasional points of contact with Greek myth. The general dependence of the Latin on the Greek poets for their mythology is as clear to him as it is to us.

To bring out his view distinctly, I have dwelt especially on philosophical interpretations; but the strength of the argument is in the accumulation of detail. No doubt it is "induction by simple enumeration"; but the very facility of the process is in favour of the result. The minds of the theorists were flexible and imaginative enough to disentangle sympathetically the web of imagination in a mythology first spontaneously and then consciously and artistically poetic. All that we need to add to the generalisation of Macrobius is a psychological construction from beneath. This has been supplied in recent times by Sir Edward Tylor and by Herbert Spencer, working on the records of facts concerning the minds of peoples stranded at a level of thinking more primitive than that of the predominant races of ancient Europe and Asia[1]. It is to be regretted that they imperfectly appreciated one another's work; but an interesting point that came out in the controversy

[1] See Tylor's *Primitive Culture* and Spencer's *Principles of Sociology*, vol. i.

between them is the concession that the generalisation seemed almost to emerge of itself from the facts. Like their ancient precursors in the study of myth, they were not wanting in a real gift of fancy, which enabled them to follow the processes of a more primitive intelligence than that of the medium in which they lived.

Both have shown how, starting from various phenomena such as dreams, trances, reflexions, shadows and so forth, the savage mind sought in the idea of a separable self the means of explaining the subjective life, of which man, as he emerged from a merely animal condition, gradually became aware in contrast with his objective activities among things. This self by degrees came to be imagined as a shadowy "ghost-soul." Since it appeared to depart and return (for example, in sleep and waking life) it was thought of as surviving the body, and at length was conceived to live on indefinitely. As the ghost, it became the object of a cult, being supposed still to have power. The cult consisted in offering to it, by devices thought to confer the means of reaching it in its new abode, such words and ceremonial observances and offerings as were pleasing to a fellow-savage. Later, the ghost became a god; but Spencer and Tylor do not agree about the mode of transition from "animism" to religion.

Tylor definitely repudiates the view that the ancestral ghost as such becomes a god; and there is nothing to prevent our using his form of the "ghost-theory" as a basis for a theory of religion like that of Macrobius. The idea of the permanent soul—into which the imagination of the ghost passes—being once formed, natural objects, and at length the sun and stars and the great cosmic forces, can be supposed to be animated by a soul of their own; and it is these cosmic powers that are first called gods in the proper sense; that is, permanent living powers above humanity. When these become detached from their base, as typically in the anthropomorphic polytheism of Greece, we are, according to both Hegel and Comte, at a higher stage of religion than the "astrolatry" of the Chaldaeans. Yet, as the great gods became more humanised, the myths at first referring to cosmic processes began to appear more scandalous in contrast with the higher religion for which the gods were moral rulers; and so the philosophers looked with relative favour on the astral religion imported from the East. Though in itself something of a deviation from the normal development, this attempt to accommodate popular religion to philosophy must have helped them to reach the theory which traced the known mythological religions to a common root in the imaginative contemplation of the most impressive phenomena of the universe. That theory I believe to be on the whole sound.

Spencer supposes religion to arise in a more direct way from animism. Through the cult of ghosts thought to be specially powerful, who are usually those of kings or chiefs, the ghost becomes a god. As the other form of the ghost-theory furnishes the psychological base for Macrobius, this might have furnished the base for Euhemerus. The Cyrenaic philosopher, however, went about the explanation still more simply. Having actually seen the adoption by Alexander and his successors of that cult of the divine king which was one element in the Egyptian and Babylonian polities, he generalised it into an explanation of all religion as due to the deliberate statecraft of dynasts. This theory, as a general explanation of religion, is definitely refuted by Sextus Empiricus. How could the dynasts have thought of calling themselves "gods" in order to govern the people, if there was no popular idea of a god before? And his argument in effect disposes of a possible rehabilitation of the theory on Spencerian lines. Admitting cases of the deification of men, he points out that these always suppose the idea of some pre-existent divine power whom the person deified represents. The stock instance is that of Hercules: we find a similar position in Macrobius, who, like Sextus[1], admits at least hypothetically the existence of a man who was deified under that name, but holds that he was only one of a series of men honoured as showing forth, by their virtue, the power of the sun that was symbolised by the name[2]. The coincidence is interesting, and confirms the impression that Sextus, though he does not forget his sceptical reserve, inclined to the view that the first deifications were of cosmic powers. This is the theory that in the end prevailed among the Greeks and Romans.

The divergent theory of the Greek "atheist" had a singular fate. Seized on by the Jews who were writing "Sibylline oracles" against the Macedonian and Roman Empires, it became with them the general explanation of "the gods of the nations." All of these had been originally dynasts who, by fraud, came to be worshipped as gods. This idea passed over to the Christian Fathers,

[1] *Adv. Math.* ix. 36: *ἦν μὲν γὰρ ἐξ ἀρχῆς, ὡς φασίν, Ἀλκαῖος τοὔνομα, ὑπέδραμε δὲ τὴν Ἡρακλέους προσηγορίαν νομιζομένου παρὰ τοῖς τότε θεοῦ.*

[2] i. 20, 6: "nec aestimes Alcmena apud Thebas Boeotias natum solum vel primum Herculem nuncupatum: immo post multos atque postremus ille hac appellatione dignatus est, honoratusque hoc nomine, quia nimia fortitudine meruit nomen dei virtutem regentis."

who used it when it seemed convenient[1]; but, on European ground, it failed to predominate finally, as it had failed when Euhemerus put it forth. After the triumph of Christianity, a compromise was arrived at by which Christian poets and orators could use the names of the ancient gods very much as modern poets have conventionally used them since[2]. Yet the theory of fraud did not fail altogether to leave a trace. Dr Verrall, in an explanation, perfectly conclusive in every detail, of the famous puzzle in Dante about the birthday of Virgil[3], shows that Dante's "false and lying gods"[4] are not the gods of mythology whom he knew from the Roman poets: the names of these he uses as symbols of divine powers. They are the deified emperors. Now this tradition came down to Dante from the Jewish authors of Sibylline oracles, whose invectives were inspired by the theory of Euhemerus.

Of course the phenomena that drew the special attention of Euhemerus were themselves phenomena of religion. Analogues of them still exist, and may yet count in the future of the world; but they are outside the great normal development with which Macrobius

[1] For their alternative view, that "all the gods of the heathen are devils," they could find authority in the ascription, by Pythagoreans and Platonists, of the delight in bloodshed and the reek of sacrifice to evil "demons" who persuade men that they are gods; see Porphyry, *De Abstinentia*. They did not fail to press this point; so strongly, says Gibbon, that sometimes their attacks appear to glance at the Mosaic law.

[2] Julian, while still nominally a Christian, could without the least objection fill his panegyrical orations with mythological ornament. This is well brought out by Miss Gardner in *Julian, Philosopher and Emperor* ("Heroes of the Nations" Series, 1895).

[3] See A. W. Verrall, *Collected Essays, Classical and Modern* (Cambridge, 1913), "The Birth of Virgil" (pp. 204–218).

[4] *Inf.* i. 70–2.

dealt. Emperor-worship was never serious for religion in Europe. The stage of religion that interested the last representatives of pagan culture was the elaboration of highly imaginative theogonies suggested by the great cosmic phenomena. The proper place of this seems to be between early animism and the later definitely ethical and metaphysical theologies and philosophies to which they had themselves gone on. With the development that these were receiving in the new official religion of the Empire, they could not be expected to feel any sympathy; but in the reasoned statement of a fundamental creed the two parties would scarcely have differed.

Book ii, to which we must now turn, shows us very clearly that the educated world of antiquity had found itself, quite apart from the appearance of a new religion, driven politically down a way that it did not desire to go. The *dicta* or *dicteria* quoted nearly all go back to the republican times, or, at the latest, to the beginning of the monarchy when there was still an interest in the struggle between the old and the new. In the Latin as in the Greek portion of the Empire, newer events and persons were as far as possible ignored in literature except by those who set themselves expressly to write the annals or celebrate the things of their own time. Already certain limited periods were "classical"; and we have followed the tradition. Yet, while the unloved new institutions were by preference left out of view, a certain advance in civilisation was quite recognised against indiscriminate praisers of "the good old times." The guests at the banquet of Praetextatus do not fear to compare themselves, not altogether to their own disadvantage, with the guests in Plato's *Symposium*.

The most vivid of all the stories told is that of the

Roman knight Laberius who wrote mimes, and who was compelled by Julius Caesar to appear on the stage as a performer in a mime. His prologue is given in full[1]; and finally the verse which he threw out during the action is quoted: "Necesse est multos timeat quem multi timent." At this, it is said, all the people turned their eyes on the dictator, who was obliged to sit helpless under the taunt[2]. Similarly, there is an essentially derisory tone in the anecdotes that tell how various birds were taught to salute Augustus, when he returned victorious from Actium, with the words, "Ave Caesar."

Here it seems in more than one way appropriate to refer to another work written on the occasion of the Saturnalia—the *Caesars* of Julian. For this very lively and audacious piece, though written by an emperor, retains the hostile or derisory tone to the founders of the monarchy; and, though written by the restorer of the ancient cult, reminds us a little of Aristophanes or Lucian in its treatment of Olympus[3]. It was evidently intended as a manifesto against the apotheosis, and may even have been meant to reassure the Christians that one pagan institution at least would not be revived. Like Shakespeare[4], Julian makes Caesar something of a braggart. Alexander, contesting his claim to the first place among the divine successors of the god Quirinus,

[1] ii. 7, 3.

[2] ii. 7, 5: "quo dicto universitas populi ad solum Caesarem oculos et ora convertit, notantes impotentiam eius hac dicacitate lapidatam."

[3] I cannot help feeling an underlying irony in Julian's use of the art of rhetoric to defend the "will to believe" in the miracle wrought by the image of the Mother of the Gods on arriving at Rome (Or. v. 161 AB). The orator is pleased with his debating point.

[4] Cf. *As You Like It*, Act v. Sc. 2: "Caesar's thrasonical brag"; also *Cymbeline*, Act iii. Sc. 1.

reproaches him with subduing the Germans and the Gauls in order to attack his own country[1]. Silenus, the jester, who is allowed to philosophise pretty often, tells him that he might make himself the master of Rome, but that he could not, with all his acting of philanthropy, make himself loved[2]. If Brutus and Cassius were driven out of the city, it was not for love of Caesar, but through the bribery of the people in his will. Augustus is put out of countenance by being called an image-maker[3]—that is, introducer of little images of himself as new gods; and there is a touch of sarcasm in the allusion to what his biographer says about the glance of his eyes, which he prided himself on thinking to be like that of the Sun-god[4].

Not everything in the speeches need be taken as considered opinion; but, all allowance being made for dialectic and rhetoric, "Julian is rather serious," as he acknowledges in apologising for a certain want of facility in jesting. In his essentially republican ethics[5], he is following a tradition represented by Marcus Aurelius among the emperors before him. To Marcus the gods, in the competition for honours among the deified kings, give the prize (voting by ballot). The prize is for "good

[1] *Caesares*, 324 A: σὺ δὲ τοὺς Γερμανοὺς καὶ Γαλάτας κατεπολέμησας, ἐπὶ τὴν πατρίδα τὴν σεαυτοῦ παρασκευαζόμενος, οὗ τί γένοιτ' ἂν χεῖρον ἢ μιαρώτερον;

[2] *Ibid.* 332 A: Ἀλλὰ τοῦτο μέν, εἶπεν, ἐδυνήθης· ἀγαπηθῆναι δὲ ὑπ' αὐτῶν οὐχ οἷός τε ἐγένου, καὶ ταῦτα πολλὴν μὲν ὑποκρινάμενος ὥσπερ ἐν δράματι καὶ σκηνῇ φιλανθρωπίαν, αἰσχρῶς δὲ αὐτοὺς πάντας κολακεύων.

[3] κοροπλάθος (332 D).

[4] *Ibid.* 309 A B: εἶναί τε ἤθελε τὰς βολὰς τῶν ὀμμάτων ὁποῖός ἐστιν ὁ μέγας Ἥλιος· οὐδένα γὰρ οἱ τῶν πάντων ἀντιβλέπειν ἠξίου.

[5] Caesar himself, while taking credit for his clemency, admits the justice of his fate (321 C): ἐγὼ καὶ τοῖς πολεμίοις συνέγνων· ἔπαθον γοῦν ὑπ' αὐτῶν ὅσα ἐμέλησε τῇ Δίκῃ.

conduct." Julian, himself more of a man of genius than Marcus, would evidently have liked to go beyond the Romans to the Greeks and give the first place to Alexander, whom he treats throughout sympathetically, representing him as repentant for his faults. In the end, the deifications are tacitly abolished. Cronos and Zeus consult together and tell the competitors to choose each his own divinity. Caesar wanders about at a loss till Ares and Aphrodite take pity on him and call him to them. To Julian himself, as Hermes tells him after relating the whole story of the banquet in heaven, the Sun-god Mithras is assigned as his divine patron. The policy of the Emperor is here evidently set forth in symbol. The only divine king recognised henceforth will be King Helios, popularly represented in the many gods, and philosophically interpreted as the "intellectual sun"; but with this established religion is to be combined complete freedom of worship secured by law.

No doubt Macrobius and his friends would have liked this policy to succeed; but, living a generation later, they are no longer concerned with the practical question. They hold their offices at the will of a Christian emperor, though the time has not yet come when all are obliged to profess the emperor's religion. It seems like a preparation for the next age when they turn from speculation about the nature of the gods and stories of the old time to the critical study of Virgil. The beginning of Book iii, with the end of Book ii, is lost: at the place where it opens, the topic under discussion is the poet's knowledge of religious rites. In the course of the discussion there are curious pieces of antiquarianism; as, for example, the explanation of a passage by the old notion that the gods can be constrained to hear prayers and to be worshipped with due rites against their will. Juno is made to complain that she has suffered this from Aeneas[1]. Those who are specially interested in "taboos" may find in a saying quoted from Pompeius Festus a possible line of transition from religious ritual to ethical religion[2]. Virgil's learning in ritual is proved by his coincidences with Varro[3]. That he used his profound knowledge of archaic ritual allusively, like a poet, Macrobius knows quite well and approves of it as right. When he says that "eximius," applied to a victim, is not a poetical epithet[4], he means "merely poetical": Virgil knew the correct priestly terms, and was not indulging in otiose ornament.

Discussing the departure of the gods from Troy (*Aen.* ii. 351–2), Praetextatus (to whom the exposition has again been assigned) states various conjectures on the name of the god of Rome. The true name of the city, he admits, was never known even to the most learned; the Romans taking care that enemies should not do to them what they knew that they had often done to the cities of enemies[5]. Then he cites from antiquarians the quaint formulae by which the gods of a city were invited to leave it and take up their abode among the Romans, and the city itself and its army "devoted": the formula of devotion could be pronounced only by dictators and

[1] iii. 1, 4.

[2] iii. 3, 10: "secundum Pompeium Festum *religiosi sunt, qui facienda et vitanda discernunt.*"

[3] iii. 4, 1–6.

[4] iii. 5, 6: "*eximii* quoque in sacrificiis vocabulum non poeticum ἐπίθετον sed sacerdotale nomen est."

[5] iii. 9, 5: "ipsius vero urbis nomen etiam doctissimis ignoratum est, caventibus Romanis, ne quod saepe adversus urbes hostium fecisse se noverant, idem ipsi quoque hostili evocatione paterentur, si tutelae suae nomen divulgaretur."

generals[1]. There follows a disputation in which Euangelus states the case that can be made against Virgil's sacerdotal learning; Praetextatus replying on each point[2].

There is a gap between the twelfth chapter and the thirteenth, and we find ourselves in an argument by Caecina (one of the two Albini) against Horus, who is here presented as an ascetic philosopher rebuking the luxury of the time. The speaker maintains that, incomparably inferior as the men of the present are to those of that age, the existing luxury was exceeded by the great period of the Republic[3]. In proof, he quotes tangible facts from records. The argument is taken up by Furius, who carries it back to the time of the Scipios. Undoubtedly those that won the empire could not have done it without abundance of virtues, but they were also not without vices, of which some have been corrected in our age by sobriety of manners[4]. Modern readers will find it excessive austerity in these Roman pagans to disapprove of the freer manners of their ancestors that permitted boys and girls to learn to dance. Even distinguished men of mature years, it is noted as a scandal, prided themselves on dancing well[5]. The results are given of much research on that favourite subject of declamation, the luxury of the fish-ponds. By recorded facts about certain fishes, it is shown that the quest for them was a more serious affair in earlier times than in later[6]. As proof of the excessive luxury of the old times, the history of the sumptuary laws is recalled. These, beginning at Rome far back in the Republic, and proved insufficient, had to be extended

[1] iii. 9, 9. [2] iii. cc. 10–12. [3] iii. 13, 16.
[4] iii. 14, 2. [5] iii. 14, 14–15.
[6] iii. 16, 9 (on the size and price of the mullet): "at nunc et maioris ponderis passim videmus et pretia haec insana nescimus."

and applied to all Italy. Is it then, Furius asks, the mark of a sober age that such laws should be needed? Not so: there is an old saying that good laws are occasioned by bad customs[1]. The present age is so temperate that it does not even know by name delicacies on which a limitation of price was imposed by the dictator Sulla[2].

The discourse of Furius is interrupted by the coming in of dessert, and this leads to a discussion on the kinds of nuts and the derivation of their names. From nuts the discourse (attributed to the commentator Servius) proceeds to a classification of fruits in general[3].

At the opening of Book iv there is another gap. The discussion on Virgil has in the meantime been resumed. The poet's mastery of every kind of figure classified by the writers on the arts of expressing and appealing to the emotions is illustrated with copious detail. This is not the most readable book; but the part that has been preserved is short; and, if it does nothing else, it shows with what patience a technical rhetoric had been worked out on the basis of a psychology of the feelings.

Book v opens with an argument that Virgil is as much an orator as a poet. All the four kinds of eloquence recognised as characteristic in different Roman writers are to be found in him; and it might even be said that he alone has mixed in his work the ten different styles of the ten Attic orators[4]. In a passage of deliberately heightened tone, the speaker is made to say that this poet has no less variety and brings no less harmonious a music out of dissonance than nature herself, the mother of all things. His poetic work, if you know its beauties

[1] iii. 17, 10: "vetus verbum *leges* inquit *bonae ex malis moribus procreantur*."

[2] iii. 17, 12. [3] iii. cc. 18–20. [4] v. 1, 20.

in detail, will resemble in your eyes the divine work of the world. To the speech of Eusebius, Euangelus raises an objection that gives the next speaker, Eustathius, an easy case to answer, and leads on to more distinctively literary criticism. How could this countryman from the neighbourhood of Mantua, born of rustic parents and brought up in rustic surroundings, have the slightest knowledge of Grecian letters?[1] Eustathius of course has no difficulty in proving that the Mantuan was one of the most learned of poets. Himself a Greek[2], he speaks of Virgil as "your poet," and recounts in his honour—quite in accordance with the ideas of the Romans—how he has reproduced Theocritus in his *Eclogues*, Hesiod in his *Georgics*, and so forth; but especially how he has appropriated the matter of Homer to the subject of his own Epic. Next he begins an exposition, which he is asked by Avienus to continue more systematically, of Virgil's definite imitations or translations from Homer. To take a verse from Homer, Avienus compares with robbing Jupiter of his thunderbolt or Hercules of his club: this the Roman poet has done so as to make what he has taken appear his own[3].

In the systematic exposition, parallel passages are given in profusion, first to show simply how Virgil makes Homer's verses his own, little comment being added[4]. Then the speaker shows by new examples[5] how in some passages the Roman poet is richer in virtue of closer observation of nature or deeper psychology. Having quoted other examples to illustrate equality of splendour in the two poets[6], he goes on to cases where Virgil is distinctly inferior, sometimes so inferior that the com-

[1] v. 2, 1. [2] v. 3, 2; cf. 3, 16. [3] v. 3, 16.
[4] v. cc. 4–10. [5] v. c. 11. [6] v. c. 12.

parison almost raises a blush[1]. There is no need, he says, to spend elaborate explanation on showing the greater life and vigour of Homer in describing the onset of battle[2]. On the simile of the eagle and serpent (*Aen.* xi. 751–6, taken from *Il.* xii. 200–7) the severe criticism is passed that the soul has gone and all that is left in the Latin verses is a lifeless body[3].

There follows a technical discussion in which it is shown that Virgil carried his imitation of Homer so far that he imitated what are wrongly blamed by some as defects of metre: the beginning of a line with a short syllable, the use of a short syllable for a long in the middle of a line, and the ending with redundant syllables. Like Homer, he sometimes introduces a line that might be prose; he successfully follows him in the skilful use of repetitions; and he shows how much he admired the Homeric double epithets by imitating them[4]. We are given as examples, not of course literal translations of the epithets cited, but epithets formed on the Homeric model—*malesuada fides, auricomi rami, centumgeminus Briareus*[5].

In the Catalogues, and in the management of the personages introduced in them, the critic finds the Latin

[1] v. 13, 26.

[2] v. 13, 27. Here we come upon one of the many cases where no attempt is made to keep up consistently the illusion of dialogue: "quanta sit differentia utriusque loci lectori aestimandum relinquo."

[3] v. 13, 30: "his praetermissis, quae animam parabolae dabant, velut exanimum in Latinis versibus corpus remansit."

[4] v. 14, 7: "Homerica quoque epitheta quantum sit admiratus imitando confessus est....κυανοχαῖτα Ποσειδάων, Διὸς νεφεληγερέταο,...et mille talium vocabulorum, quibus velut sideribus micat divini carminis variata maiestas."

[5] v. 14, 8: "adde et *fumiferam noctem*, et quicquid in singulis paene versibus diligens lector agnoscit."

poet decidedly inferior. Homer gives the series of the ships and whence they came in a regular order; and the heroes make their appearance in the poem in such a way that we can distinguish one from the other. Virgil observes no order in citing the names from the different parts of Italy; introduces names of apparently important heroes and then tells us no actions of theirs, glorious or otherwise; and in some cases has his persons killed over again by different hands. In contrast with Homer's simplicity of narrative in the Catalogue itself, he deliberately varies the literary form of the introductions. Here the critic expresses his personal preference for the manner of Homer[1], but allows that Virgil might almost be said to have improved on his art in accumulating names[2].

It has taken modern discoveries to enable us to understand this difference. We now know that there was a real siege of Troy; and no doubt there was some actual tradition behind the catalogue of the Achaeans on one side and of the Trojan auxiliaries on the other. In the later books of the *Aeneid,* recounting the battles on Italian soil, there could only be artificial combinations of archaeological detail brought into a semblance of unity by imitation of Homer; for of course the tradition about the coming of Aeneas was late. The future predicted for him in the *Iliad* is thought to have referred originally to the foundation of some new kingdom in the neighbourhood of Troy. That Achaeans and Trojans alike were "Greeks," modern research has proved; but

[1] v. 15, 16: "has copias fortasse putat aliquis divinae illi simplicitati praeferendas, sed nescio quo modo Homerum repetitio illa unice decet."

[2] v. 15, 18–19.

the knowledge of this, though some traces of it are discoverable in ancient authors, had passed out of the tradition used by Virgil as by the Greek tragedians.

Both poets, the critic proceeds, for the relief of the reader introduce agreeable fables into their catalogues[1]. Virgil is especially to be admired for the digressions in the *Georgics* from the dry precepts of agriculture. Both abound in apophthegms. Virgil sometimes departs from Homer in his theological doctrine, be this by accident or of his own will. Homer never mentions fortune, but always ascribes events to the decree of fate. Virgil, on the contrary, ascribes omnipotence to fortune; whereas even the philosophers who name her make her the subordinate minister of providence[2]. In many details also of myth and story he departs from Homer. For example, Homer never mentions the judgment of Paris[3].

It is unfortunate, says Eustathius, that Virgil had not Homer or some other Greek model to follow in assigning the causes for the beginning of the war in the seventh book[4]. For want of an adequate cause, he has had to set in motion his Furies from hell and snakes and bacchanals. "Some other model," he says advisedly; for in the fourth book the poet has followed not Homer

[1] v. 16, 1–4.

[2] v. 16, 8: "in non nullis ab Homerica secta haud scio casune an sponte desciscit. fortunam Homerus nescire maluit, et soli decreto, quam μοῖραν vocat, omnia regenda committit adeo, ut hoc vocabulum τύχη in nulla parte Homerici voluminis nominetur. contra Vergilius non solum novit et meminit, sed omnipotentiam quoque eidem tribuit, quam et philosophi, qui eam nominant, nihil sua vi posse, sed decreti sive providentiae ministram esse voluerunt."

[3] v. 16, 10: "nullam commemorationem de iudicio Paridis Homerus admittit." This shows that Macrobius, with the Alexandrian critics, rejected *Il.* xxiv. 25–30 as an interpolation.

[4] v. 17, 4.

but Apollonius Rhodius, from whom he borrowed the story of Medea, adapting it to the episode of Dido. But here special tribute is paid to the power of the Roman poet. Everybody knows the love-story of Dido as related by Virgil to be historically false; and yet all are moved by it. It has been taken over from poetry as a subject for all the arts, and has never ceased to be represented on the stage both in action and in song.

The attempt to imitate Pindar, whom Horace confessed to be inimitable, is declared a failure[1]. In Virgil's description of an eruption of Aetna (*Aen.* iii. 574 ff.), suggested by a famous passage of Pindar (*Pyth.* i. 40 ff.), the critic finds nothing but a sound of words. Pindar describes things really seen: Virgil picks up images of things neither seen nor heard, and ends in monstrosity[2].

From things known, as he says, to all or some of the Romans, the critic now comes to obscure allusions drawn from the less familiar parts of Grecian letters[3]. The learning at his disposal ranges over the dramatists, tragic and comic, the lyrists and the historians; many fragments of lost works being preserved. At the end of the dissertation, we are told that the grammarians did not know from what author Virgil had taken his description of Apollo as the prophet of Zeus (*Aen.* iii. 251), but ascribed it to the invention of the poet. Eustathius ventures to affirm that it is from Aeschylus,

[1] v. 17, 7–14. Macrobius has only three or four references to Horace, and none to Ovid. Ennius as well as Lucretius he knows well; and he quotes Catullus.

[2] v. 17, 14; cf. 17, 8: "eius modi sententias et verba molitus est, ut Pindaro quoque ipso, qui nimis opima et pingui facundia existimatus est, insolentior hoc quidem in loco tumidiorque sit."

[3] v. 18, 1: "fuit enim hic poeta ut scrupulose et anxie, ita dissimulanter et clanculo doctus, ut multa transtulerit, quae unde translata sint difficile sit cognitu."

the highest name among the writers of tragedy[1], and quotes in support of his opinion two lines from a lost drama called the *Sacerdotes* and one from the *Eumenides*.

After the exposition of the poet's debts to the Greeks, Praetextatus calls upon the two Albini, Furius and Caecina, the most learned men of the age[2], to deal similarly with his debts to the ancient Roman writers. This is the subject of Book vi.

Furius begins with an excellent defence of Virgil's use of his reading, treated by some as robbery. From the old comic poet Afranius, he quotes the reply made to those who accused him of taking many things from Menander. "Not only have I taken from Menander," he confesses, "but from any one else, even a Latin writer, who had anything which was to my purpose and which I did not think I could express better[3]." Of course Furius adds that Virgil always gave some distinctive turn to that which he annexed.

Among the borrowed phrases are two famous ones: "cunctando restituit rem" (*Aen.* vi. 847) from Ennius[4], and "non omnia possumus omnes" (*Eclogue* viii. 63) from Lucilius[5]. The most elaborate comparison is between various details in the description of a pestilence at the

[1] v. 22, 12: "in talibus locis grammatici excusantes imperitiam suam inventiones has ingenio magis quam doctrinae Maronis adsignant, nec dicunt, eum ab aliis mutuatum, ne nominare cogantur auctores. sed adfirmo, doctissimum vatem etiam in hoc Aeschylum, eminentissimum tragoediarum scriptorem, secutum."

[2] vi. 1, 1: "viros inter omnes nostra aetate longe doctissimos." More than a century later, an Albinus was accused, along with Boethius, of conspiracy against Theodoric. See Gibbon, *Roman Empire*, ch. xxxix, ed. Bury, vol. iv. p. 200. "The senator Albinus was accused and already convicted on the presumption of *hoping*, as it was said, the liberty of Rome."

[3] vi. 1, 4. [4] vi. 1, 23. [5] vi. 1, 35.

end of the third book of the *Georgics* and the description of the plague at Athens in the sixth book of Lucretius[1]. It is not pointed out that this last is taken from Thucydides, though Macrobius has references to Thucydides elsewhere. If any doubt has been felt that Virgil had closely studied and was profoundly influenced by Lucretius, the doubt is completely resolved by the exact demonstrations of Macrobius. It is shown besides that Virgil has little touches suggested by Cicero[2]; and that in some cases he has not borrowed directly from Homer, as is commonly thought, but owes his turns of expression to imitations of Homeric passages by rough old Latin poets like Ennius. For the style of these Furius apologises[3], and then hands over the subject to Caecina to continue from his own memory.

Caecina proceeds to show that the poet has been as diligent in his search of the ancient writers for particular words that suited his purpose as in his adaptation of verses and passages: it is the loss of curiosity about antiquity that makes his words appear new or singular. Among epithets thought to be of Virgil's invention, but really drawn from the ancients, are "Gradivus" for Mars and "Mulciber" for Vulcan[4]. The copious learning here is of more interest on the whole to philologists than to general students of literature; as is also the

[1] vi. 2, 7: "ipsius vero pestilentiae, quae est in tertio Georgicorum, color totus et liniamenta paene omnia tracta sunt de descriptione pestilentiae, quae est in sexto Lucretii."

[2] vi. 2, 33–34.

[3] vi. 3, 9: "nemo ex hoc loco viles putet veteres poetas, quod versus eorum scabri nobis videntur." Cf. vi. 8, 9: "nam quia saeculum nostrum ab Ennio et omni bibliotheca vetere descivit, multa ignoramus, quae non laterent, si veterum lectio nobis esset familiaris."

[4] vi. 5, 1.

remainder of the book, in which the commentator Servius is the chief speaker. The most interesting development for literary criticism is in the seventh chapter, where the art of Virgil in apparent understatement is brought out; as in calling Busiris, the Egyptian king who is said to have offered up human victims, "inlaudatus," and the Stygian pool "inamabilis."

Book vii, which is the last, is of more special interest in relation to philosophy, and forms a transition (whether intentional or not) to the Commentary on Scipio's Dream. In the first chapter, a question is raised about introducing philosophy at banquets. When we read that to exclude it altogether would be to exclude all the virtues, we perceive how decisively the tradition of considering it as "moral philosophy" had been impressed during the Stoic and Epicurean period. Yet the questions we find actually discussed are scientific and speculative; and that these are now usually abstruse, is evident from the general agreement that at banquets philosophy should be present only in moderation. When philosophers at a feast are in very small proportion to the other guests, and cannot hope to interest the company, they do best to be silent on their own topics. Even when there seems to be a place for them to come in, they should not talk about the deeper things and the knotty questions, but should start rather those that are useful and at the same time easy.

The rules of social intercourse laid down are those of a decidedly amiable society. Questions should be put about a person's knowledge or experience that will enable him to make a good figure by answering them, and so will give him pleasure. From anything contumelious, the wise ought to refrain at all times, and all ought to refrain at banquets. Jests should be made and received without offence; and there is an art of disguising compliments under the appearance of pointing out faults. Such rules about convivialities, says Eustathius, addressing the Romans as a Greek, were not disdained by Aristotle and Plutarch and "your own Apuleius"[1].

A discussion follows in which first Disarius, a doctor, makes a speech commending a simple diet as the most healthful. Eustathius replies on behalf of variety; introducing a passage from the Αἶγες of Eupolis, remarkable for its profuse botanical vocabulary, in which goats boast of the varied kinds of herbs that they eat[2]. Thus if "dumb animals" were a model for us, as the simplifiers appear to think, the case for simplicity would not be proved. But how can we take them for models when, Homer being the witness, pestilence falls on them first? Fables apart, they are shorter-lived than men; and those that are said to be long-lived are quite as greedy. Eustathius, however, ends by describing himself as a lover of temperance reluctantly arguing as a dialectical disputant because he has been pressed to take the other side. He has ventured to say a word for pleasure in eating; but it is agreed on both sides that anything to which the name of luxury can be applied is incompatible with the philosophic life.

The miscellaneous physical and physiological discussion that follows, in which heat and cold are taken as principles of explanation, shows what an authority Aristotle[3] had become in science. A passing mention

[1] vii. 3, 24.
[2] vii. 5, 9.
[3] vii. 6, 16: "cuius inventis nec ipsa natura dissentit."

of the complete disuse of cremation has some historical interest[1].

A topic more closely related to philosophy is the psychology of the senses. Disarius combines the observation of Aristotle, that the brain itself is insensitive, with the sound Platonic view (rejected by Aristotle), that the co-ordination of the senses and the sending out of impulses nevertheless have their seat in the brain. It does not at all follow, because the brain has not sense, that it cannot direct the senses. The *anima*, present there, is without sense (as distinguished from power to relate the senses to one another); but it is that which, through the brain, makes the composite being, the *animal*, sensitive. Animation of the body is caused and directed from the brain and the spinal marrow through the nerves, by means of the *spiramentum* that permeates them from the ventricles of the brain outward to the muscles. The *anima* itself is beyond all body[2].

This is Neo-Platonic doctrine in a relatively popular and adaptable form. The *spiramentum* is of course the "animal spirit" which continued to be part of orthodox physiology till modern times. It was taken over from the Stoics and assigned a place within the mechanism of the body, but deposed from the supreme position which it held in their doctrine. Renewed metaphysical thinking had made it impossible for the educated thought of a later age to accept such a crude mode of accounting for either mind or organism as sufficed for Seneca; who has no explanation or even description to give except that the unity we find to be characteristic of them is the

[1] vii. 7, 5: "licet urendi corpora defunctorum usus nostro saeculo nullus sit."

[2] vii. 9, 16.

tension of a *spiritus* or air[1]. The *anima* for Macrobius is no longer a "breath," but the unity of life and sense (and, in man, of thought) expressly recognised as something unique and not definable in corporeal terms. At the same time, through the advance of physiological science, the material conditions are more accurately defined than they could be in the time of Plato or Aristotle.

The discussions that follow on the causes of baldness and grey hairs and of blushing and pallor, and on various "natural questions" about honey, wine, oil, the properties of sea-water, etc., need not be set forth in detail. One or two points illustrate the ideals of the more rigorous philosophic sects. An expert on the pontifical law, Ateius Capito, was evidently tinged with Pythagorean doctrines, since he laid down the rule not to carve the image of a god on a ring[2]. Caecina quotes from him an explanation, entirely from utilitarian causes, of the custom of wearing a ring on the fourth finger of the left hand. Further on in the dialogue, Horus mentions that he has only one garment and no slave, and does everything for himself. He needed, however, the practical instruction of a sailor, who told him that fresh water was better than sea-water for washing his cloak[3]. Incidentally, Eustathius is allowed to question the authority of Aristotle[4].

[1] See *Naturales Quaestiones*, ii. 6, 6: "esse autem unitatem in aëre vel ex hoc intellegi potest, quod corpora nostra inter se cohaerent: quid enim est aliud, quod tenet illa, quam spiritus? quid est aliud, quo animus noster agitatur? quis est illi motus nisi intentio? quae intentio nisi ex unitate? quae unitas, nisi haec esset in aëre?"

[2] vii. 13, 11: "nefas esse...deorum formas insculpi anulis."

[3] vii. 13, 17–18.

[4] vii. 13, 21: "Aristoteles enim ut non nulla alia, magis acute quam vere ista disseruit."

Proceeding from the discussion of the properties of water, he asks why the appearance of things is modified when they are seen in water instead of through the air. Disarius in answer sets forth the Epicurean theory that images are constantly being thrown off from the surfaces of bodies, and that by means of these we see the things: the denser medium of water modifies the images as they pass. The discourse of Eustathius that follows is one more evidence of the increased clearness of thought regarding mental processes. It shows a definite understanding of the active element in sight. The passively received phantasms of the Epicureans, the speaker proves, cannot explain vision. The act of seeing requires, besides sense, the aid of memory and reason. These involve comparisons of the impressions of sight with those of the other senses. It is only by insisting on this that the arguments of the Academics against the possibility of knowledge can be refuted[1]. We know that a certain kind of thing (for example, an apple) which the reason has inferred from the visual image by memories, is actually there, when we have tested the inference successively by the other senses (in this case, smell, touch and taste) and found it correct.

The speech of Eustathius, received with applause by all the rest, not excepting Euangelus, somehow provokes Disarius; perhaps because the speaker, to arrive at his sounder psychology, had brought in Plato's fancy that the eye sends out a light of its own to meet the light from the object of vision. Disarius does not mention this, but directly attacks philosophy as claiming for herself provinces that belong to the other arts. Take, for example, Plato's laughable mistake in saying that

[1] vii. 14, 21.

food and drink go down by different ways, the first through the gullet and the second through the trachea. The true account has been set forth by Erasistratus, "medicorum veterum nobilissimus[1]." Disarius quotes and comments on the passage of Erasistratus, adding a remark which he thinks useful for philosophers when they have occasion to refer to the sciences[2].

Eustathius begins his reply by a compliment. He had always classed Disarius himself among philosophers as well as physicians. But now, he continues, you seem to commit to oblivion something accepted by the consent of the human race, that philosophy is the art of arts and discipline of disciplines, working downwards by rational methods. Medicine is at the other extreme, dealing with that part of physics where conjecture rather than reason reigns[3]; and that it should rise up against philosophy is an act of parricidal daring. Then he goes on to defend Plato dialectically, citing the testimony of poets more ancient than the philosopher. Obviously such a debating defence of a known error is to be taken only as part of the fashionable game of arguing on every side in turn. The serious reply in that age was already a commonplace; that knowledge had grown, and that the early philosophers wrote before any special sciences had been established.

After this display of skill, Euangelus, "envying and mocking the glory of the Greeks," proposes the question,

[1] vii. 15, 3.

[2] vii. 15, 13: "vides satius fuisse philosophorum omnium principi alienis abstinere quam minus nota proferre."

[3] vii. 15, 15: "medicina autem physicae partis extrema faex est, cui ratio est cum testeis terrenisque corporibus, sed quid rationem nominavi, cum magis apud ipsam regnet coniectura quam ratio?"

Which came first, the egg or the hen? Disarius has no objection to taking up the problem, and defends both sides in succession, leaving the choice of the right solution to Euangelus. Defending the thesis that the egg came first, he makes use of the position admitted in all the schools, that in the order of genesis the imperfect comes before the perfect, and only reaches perfection through the additions made by art and time[1]. The "rationes seminales" which are in the simple egg, he adds in explanation of the process, are as it were the elements of the complex fowl[2]. We may see in this an anticipation of Spencer's "physiological units"; as we may see in what is recorded of a lost treatise of the early Stoic, Sphaerus, *περὶ σπέρματος*, an anticipation of Darwin's "pangenesis[3]." And this is not to consider the scientific theories of the ancients too curiously; for modern biology, in spite of immensely greater knowledge of the organism in detail, is still no less an affair of speculative conjecture on these ultimate questions than the biology known to Sphaerus or Macrobius.

[1] vii. 16, 3: "semper enim, quod incipit, imperfectum adhuc et informe est, et ad perfectionem sui per procedentis artis et temporis additamenta formatur."

[2] vii. 16, 5: "nam sicut elementa prius extiterunt, et ita reliqua corpora de commixtione eorum creata sunt, ita rationes seminales, quae in ovo sunt, si venialis erit ista translatio, velut quaedam gallinae elementa credenda sunt."

[3] Diog. Laert. vii. 159: *καὶ ἀφ' ὅλων δὲ τῶν σωμάτων αὐτό [τὸ σπέρμα] φασι καταφέρεσθαι οἱ περὶ τὸν Σφαῖρον· πάντων γοῦν γεννητικὸν εἶναι τῶν τοῦ σώματος μερῶν.*

III

SCIPIO'S DREAM

THE commentary of Macrobius on the *Somnium Scipionis* of Cicero is dedicated, like the *Saturnalia*, to his son. In form it resembles the commentaries, dating from the fifth century, of Syrianus and Proclus. Short passages from the book commented on are quoted verbatim, and a circumstantial discussion, philosophical not philological, added. Not only the form but the matter resembles that of the "Platonic successors" at Athens. Macrobius does not indeed refer to Iamblichus or his disciples, whose influence so far may have travelled exclusively eastward; but for the rest his authorities are the same, and his references to Plotinus and Porphyry are frequent. Plotinus[1] he puts on a level with Plato himself.

This portion of Cicero's treatise *On the Republic*, he begins by explaining, corresponds to the Vision of Er in Plato's. In both treatises, after the need of justice for the State and for every community of men has been proved, a proof of the immortality of the soul is added; this being the condition on which some fruit of the love of justice may remain when the bond between soul and body has been dissolved. To this proof, both philosophers found that they must add further the description of a local habitation for departed souls. And because some derided the story in Plato of one who came to life again from the funeral pile and reported what he had

[1] See the reference, bk i. 8, 5: "inter philosophiae professores cum Platone princeps."

seen between two lives, Cicero adopted in preference the form of a dream. In a dream, the younger Scipio has his destiny revealed to him by the ancestral souls whom he meets in the heaven of the fixed stars. As in Plato's description, so also in Cicero's, much is said that belongs to astronomy. One reason for writing a commentary is to make it clear why this should be so in books of which the proper subject is the government of human life.

Macrobius, like Proclus later, feels himself under the necessity of defending the use of myths or fables to illustrate philosophical truth. He begins by a reply to an Epicurean, Colotes, who in a written argument, as well as in much vituperative speech, maintained that a philosopher, as professing to teach truth, should have allowed himself no kind of fiction at all[1]. The defence consists in distinguishing between kinds of fiction permissible and not permissible.

Literary fiction intended to amuse, as in comedies or stories like those of Petronius Arbiter and Apuleius, or fiction for the sake of enforcing moral precepts, as in the fables of Aesop, has its own place, but does not concern the philosopher as such. Myths with a truth behind them, but unedifying in detail, like the stories in Hesiod condemned by Plato, may also be dismissed from the argument. The only fables permitted by philosophic caution about divine things are those that convey some truth concerning souls or subordinate divine powers, without any detail that can offend the hearers. Such are the stories of Er as told by Plato and of Scipio as told by Cicero. But even this kind of fiction is no longer permissible when the discourse rises to the highest God,

[1] i. 2, 4: "ait a philosopho fabulam non oportuisse confingi, quoniam nullum figmenti genus veri professoribus conveniret."

called by the Greeks the Good (τἀγαθόν), which is the First Cause (πρῶτον αἴτιον), or to the Mind or Intellect (νοῦς) containing the original forms of things, called Ideas (ἰδέαι), which is born and proceeds from the highest God. Here only similitudes and examples are permitted[1]. And so antiquity had no image of this God; and, even in the case of the powers concealed under popular names, kept their mysteries as far as possible from vulgar contacts.

We need not follow in detail the classification of dreams into divinatory and non-divinatory; although there is some interest in noting the use of physiology, along with a psychology of association, to explain most dreams without supposing them to have anything prophetic[2]. The meaning of the dream of Scipio is briefly stated as, the immortality of happiness attained through virtue shown in preserving the commonwealth or promoting its good. The place of the vision is declared to be the galaxy. After this, we plunge into a mathematical discussion suggested by the age of fifty-six (8 × 7) which has been assigned as the critical year of Scipio's life on earth. Macrobius here introduces, for the purpose of instruction, the outlines of geometrical theory as then formulated. There are three dimensions of body; length, breadth and depth or altitude[3]. The

[1] i. 2, 15: "sic Plato, cum de τἀγαθῷ loqui esset animatus, dicere quid sit non ausus est, hoc solum de eo sciens, quod sciri quale sit ab homine non possit, solum vero ei simillimum de visibilibus solem repperit, et per eius similitudinem viam sermoni suo attollendi se ad non comprehendenda patefecit."

[2] i. 3, 3–7.

[3] i. 5, 9: "fit enim tribus dimensionibus impletis corpus solidum, quod στερεόν vocant." Cf. i. 6, 36: "nec non omnium corporum tres sunt dimensiones, longitudo latitudo profunditas: termini adnumerato effectu ultimo quattuor, punctum linea superficies et ipsa soliditas."

superficies with its lines, in distinction from the solid, is the "first incorporeal nature," but not separable from body. While speaking in general of the solid as "body," Macrobius does not confound visible and tangible body with extension, but calls this "mathematical body"[1]. The properly incorporeal is beyond extension, and begins with arithmetic. Number is prior to geometrical magnitude; it can be understood from the different numbers of lines, what geometrical forms are described[2]. Thus the first perfection of the incorporeal is in number[3]. The unit (μονάς) is not a number, but the "fons et origo numerorum[4]." From the monad as a symbol we pass, by way of an interpretation of the *Timaeus*, to a generalised statement of the Neo-Platonic "emanation." Mind, with its eternity, proceeds from the One. It remains one while creating from itself and containing innumerable kinds[5]. Soul, the next in order of emanation, is in its simplicity one and immaterial, and, while animating the immensity of the universe, undergoes no division from its own unity[6]. In these successive principles, of unity in itself, of intellect, and of that which gives life to the universe, we are dealing with the metaphysical existences that are, while things corporeal

[1] i. 6, 35: "item omnia corpora aut mathematica sunt alumna geometriae aut talia, quae visum tactumve patiantur."

[2] i. 5, 12: "a lineis enim ascenditur ad numerum tamquam ad priorem, ut intellegatur ex diversis numeris linearum, quae formae geometricae describantur."

[3] i. 5, 13: "prima est igitur perfectio incorporalitatis in numeris, et haec est, ut diximus, numerorum omnium plenitudo."

[4] i. 6, 7. We can partly understand from these definitions how the soul came to be called "a number moving itself."

[5] i. 6, 8.

[6] i. 6, 9: "vides, ut haec monas orta a prima rerum causa usque ad animam ubique integra et semper individua continuationem potestatis obtineat."

appear to be[1]. Among things corporeal are included the ethereal bodies of the stars, divine though they were according to the Aristotelian doctrine then generally accepted. We see that the pupil of the Neo-Platonists has become as clear as his masters at least on this point, that everything corporeal is to be excluded from the definition or description of properly mental existence.

Some time ago, the approach to metaphysics from the side of mathematics would have seemed more old-fashioned that it does to-day. It is not the method most characteristic of the Neo-Platonists, who were psychologists first of all. At the next step, however, Macrobius makes use of a very characteristic side of their doctrine, for which they have received little credit. He definitely appeals to Plotinus and Porphyry on behalf of the recognition of the "political virtues," as against the rigorists who would have reduced all virtue to that which they deemed the highest, namely an attitude of mental detachment from all external interests. This appeal is not to some popular expositor, but is definitely to the short book of Plotinus "On the Virtues"[2] and to the systematic classification based on this by Porphyry[3]. What he finds to his purpose is the grading of the virtues according to types of mind, or according to the stage of progress reached by individual minds. The theoretic life is indeed for Plotinus and Porphyry above the life of action; and here Macrobius follows them. This distinction in rank he finds to be recognised by Cicero when he makes the elder Scipio say that nothing *which is done on earth* is more acceptable to the God who

[1] i. 6, 19: "esse autem dicimus intelligibilia, videri esse corporalia omnia, seu divinum corpus habeant seu caducum."

[2] Enn. I. 2.

[3] *Sententiae*, 34.

rules the universe than those assemblies of men associated by the rule of right which are called States[1]. For contemplation, as illustrated especially in astronomy, is of things above the earth. This being recognised, however, Macrobius is more circumstantial in his disquisitions on political virtue than his authorities. Whether he was stimulated by any other writer, it is impossible to say; but, though this might not have been expected, he was in accordance with the movement of the time. Iamblichus is less detached, and is more circumstantial on political virtue, than his master, Porphyry; and even Proclus was not too late to show traces of renewed interest in the political activities at least of the past. A remarkable thing in the case of Iamblichus is that, in the compilation of his *Protrepticus*, he incorporated excerpts from an ethical sermon or pamphlet by an Athenian democrat of the fifth century B.C.[2]. This was exactly to the purpose of his own argument; the drift being that men cannot be deprived of their freedom except by their own fault and of their own will. Tyranny is the result of want of virtue in the multitude: so long as the people adhere to the law, no "super-man" can gain the mastery over them. A monarch, in the end, can only establish his power by restoring the laws when they have been overthrown. This was exactly the relative

[1] i. 8, 12: "iure ergo Tullius de rerum publicarum rectoribus dixit: *ubi beati aevo sempiterno fruantur*: qui ut ostenderet, alios otiosis alios negotiosis virtutibus fieri beatos, non dixit absolute, nihil esse illi principi deo acceptius quam civitates, sed adiecit *quod quidem in terris fiat*, ut eos, qui ab ipsis caelestibus incipiunt, discerneret a rectoribus civitatum, quibus per terrenos actus iter paratur ad caelum."

[2] See the restoration of the "Anonymus Iamblichi" in Diels, *Fragmente der Vorsokratiker*, II. 1, 2nd ed., pp. 629–635. The general description given by Diels is: "Eklogen einer ethisch-politischen Schrift aus der Zeit des peloponnesischen Krieges."

justification that would appeal, after the event, to philosophic republicans who saw the impossibility of anything but monarchy in the world as it then stood. We do not, however, find any argument like this in Macrobius, who ignores later history, and writes as if the world was a community of republican States.

For the future, nothing could have been better than this tradition of writing in terms of a certain ideal type of "classical" polity. The grading of modes of life by Macrobius[1] may very well have been one "source" for Dante's assignment of contemplative virtue to the Heaven of Saturn and of active virtue to the Heaven of Jupiter. This was the myth of a new world. For the myths of his own world, Macrobius goes back to Hesiod. The immortal souls of heroes that remain as guardians of mortal men[2] become, in a Latin translation cited[3], the Dii Indigetes of Roman religion[4]. Virgil, Macrobius adds, combined in a similar way philosophic truth with the fiction of the underworld[5]; but he lets us see plainly that he himself preferred the open-air fiction of Hesiod, in which the bodies are buried but the guardian souls (ἐσθλοί, ἐπιχθόνιοι, φύλακες θνητῶν ἀνθρώπων) remain above.

On the underworld as a place of punishment, he is outspoken in the manner of the Roman tradition from the time of Cicero and Caesar: we know the stories about Tartarus to be fables. He is willing, however, to allegorise them. This he does by means of the

[1] i. 12, 14. [2] *Opera et Dies*, 121 ff. [3] i. 9, 7.

[4] Cf. i. 9, 6: "nec enim de nihilo aut de vana adulatione veniebat, quod quosdam urbium conditores aut claros in re publica viros in numerum deorum consecravit antiquitas, sed Hesiodus quoque divinae subolis adsertor priscos reges cum dis aliis enumerat, hisque exemplo veteris potestatis etiam in caelo regendi res humanas adsignat officium."

[5] i. 9, 8.

Pythagorean and Platonic symbolism that made the body the tomb of the soul. At the same time, his treatment recalls that of Lucretius: he takes the torments of hell to represent the struggles, the weariness and the pains of conscience endured by those who pursue practical objects with immoderate desire. The whole treatment of the subject, with its convergence of directions diverse in origin, contrasts very favourably with Seneca's mere juxtaposition of totally different views in the book *Ad Marciam de Consolatione*; where the complete denial of anything after death[1] is followed, without any formal mediation, by the description of a heaven recalling that of Plato in the *Phaedo* or that of Scipio's Dream[2]. But Seneca, though a great moralist and a great man of letters, was scarcely at all a metaphysician. Macrobius could have removed the contradiction by his distinction between soul and composite being[3], to which we now return.

The imaginations to which he recurs to help out thought are by preference those of the philosophers, but unqualified faith in them is not commended. That Scipio, even in a dream, does not yield at once to belief, but asks questions about the reality of what he sees, is cited as a proof that he possesses, along with the other political virtues, undoubted prudence[4]. There are two

[1] Compare *Ad Marciam*, c. 19, 5, with a famous chorus in the *Troades*: "Post mortem nihil est ipsaque mors nihil," etc.

[2] The soul is set free from its impurities, clear of all subjection to fortune yet not extinct, contemplating the eternal order of the universe in conscious enjoyment of its own exemption from accident. All the souls know one another's thoughts intuitively, as in the intelligible world of Plotinus or the paradise of Dante. But, the Stoic adds, the state even of the blessed souls is not for ever: when the great deluge or conflagration comes at the end of the world-period, they too will return to their ancient elements (c. 26, 7).

[3] See above, p. 52.

[4] i. 10, 3: "quod ea, quae arbitratur, non pro compertis habet

kinds of death, Macrobius explains as a Platonist—death of the soul (the *anima*) and of the composite being (the *animal*) consisting of soul and body. What is commonly called death is release from the prison of the body and return to the true life of the soul. The true death of the soul is when, dissatisfied with the life above, and attracted by latent desire to the things below, it gradually descends, acquiring new accretions of mortality in the successive spheres, down to earth. The divisions of these spheres are described in accordance with the Aristotelian distinction between the immutable and the mutable parts of the universe[1]. From the imaginations put forth by various Platonic sects, Macrobius chooses that which he thinks most favoured by reason. No real hell is left but the troubles of this life[2], from which philosophy is the means of reascending. There is no final death of any soul: after certain stages of purgation, there is restitution for each and all to the light of perpetual life[3].

The arguments of Plotinus against suicide are taken over to confirm those of Plato and Cicero[4]. The Epicurean and Stoic permission has been quite displaced by the Orphic and Pythagorean precept that the soul shall stay where it is till God or Fate calls it hence. There is a fatal term, says Macrobius, summing up the speculative doctrine, for the bodily life. In a natural death, the soul does not quit the body, but the body, unable to continue its function, quits the soul[5]. It is not good to leave life under the impulse of a passion, that is, of

sed spreta opinione, quae minus cautis animis pro vero inolescit, quaerit discere certiora, indubitata prudentia est."

[1] i. 11, 6. [2] i. 12, 1: "huius vitae inferna." [3] i. 12, 17.

[4] i. 13, 9: "haec Platonicae sectae semina altius Plotinus exsequitur." [5] i. 13, 11–12.

something from which the soul suffers, be it hope or fear. Not in this way is the heaven of contemplation to be reached.

While doing the best he can with the vaguer literary language of Cicero or Virgil[1] about the mind of the universe or the stars, Macrobius keeps a firm hold of his own more exact doctrine. We have seen before, and may see again, that he is consciously beyond the notion of fire or breath as explaining mind or even life[2]. By Cicero, he says, the universe is well called the temple of God, to guard against the language of those who think that God is nothing but the visible heaven[3]. The divine or ethereal bodies of the stars are endowed with mind, but are not themselves minds. Below the stars, the only being that has mind (νοῦς, *mens*, *animus*) in the proper sense is man. Recapitulating Neo-Platonism, he continues: Mind emanates directly from the superabundance of the Cause, which is God; and from mind in its turn there issues soul (ψυχή, *anima*), which in man and other animals is the principle of sense and growth, in plants only of growth[4]. By the power of reason[5], mind is mediated to soul. The connexion of all things from the highest to the lowest is signified by Homer's "golden chain," stretching from heaven to earth[6].

[1] i. 14, 14. [2] i. 14, 17.

[3] i. 14, 2: "bene autem universus mundus dei templum vocatur propter illos, qui aestimant, nihil esse aliud deum nisi caelum ipsum et caelestia ista, quae cernimus."

[4] i. 14, 6: "deus, qui prima causa et est et vocatur, unus omnium, quaeque sunt quaeque videntur esse, princeps et origo est. hic superabundanti maiestatis fecunditate de se mentem creavit. haec mens, quae νοῦς vocatur, qua patrem inspicit, plenam similitudinem servat auctoris, animam vero de se creat posteriora respiciens." And so, in terms of the Plotinian "emanation," the series proceeds down to animated bodies.

[5] i. 14, 7: "quod λογικόν vocatur." [6] i. 14, 15.

From the general principles of his theology, Macrobius turns to astronomy. Starting from the galaxy, the scene of the vision, he proposes to leave aside the fables about it, and to set forth only scientific truth[1]. One in the heaven, he observes, would see not only the stars of the northern, but those also of the southern hemisphere, never seen from our part of the world[2]. The greater magnitude of the sun as compared with the earth was definitely known to the ancient astronomers: in the commentary of Macrobius, the greater magnitude of the stars is inferred. And here we find Seneca's glorification of the speculative knowledge of nature repeated with a difference. The saying of Seneca is best known in the rendering of an English poet:

Unless above himself he can
Erect himself, how poor a thing is man![3]

If taken in the sense that man rises above himself by moral virtue, this is misunderstood. The Stoic moralist has here recurred to the idea of Aristotle when he refuses to acquiesce in the view of those who said that man should confine his thoughts to things human. There is also, Aristotle replies, a divine part in man, and, by speculating on that which is eternal, he participates in immortality. Developing this thought, Seneca adds that it is not by accepting a certain belief about the universe, but by putting subtle questions about it which are perhaps insoluble, that man overleaps his mortality.

[1] i. 15, 3: "de hoc lacteo multi inter se diversa senserunt, causasque eius alii fabulosas, naturales alii protulerunt: sed nos fabulosa reticentes ea tantum, quae ad naturam eius visa sunt pertinere, dicemus."

[2] i. 16, 7.

[3] Samuel Daniel; cf. Sen. *Nat. Quaest.* i. Praef. 5: "O quam contempta res est homo, nisi supra humana surrexerit!"

With an evident allusion to this passage of Seneca, Macrobius modifies the thought: only speculative science, he declares, raises a man above his own nature—or rather, makes him truly a man. To those not thus raised, the stars taken singly would appear scarcely to equal the flame of one torch[1].

But we are not allowed to rest long in physics. As with Plato, the cause of motion is the incorporeal essence of the soul; and, as with Plotinus, it is this that fabricates body[2]. Macrobius, however, while showing a real grasp of the system, does not follow his Greek masters to the limits of their thought. We do not find in him their subtler theories either of the One beyond being or of incorporeal "matter" as the bare possibility of body. His simplified series of terms begins with God and descends through the stages of communicated intellect and animation to the visible bodies that compose the universe. Yet his literary language is used to convey a meaning not identical with that of Seneca or Lucan, who float in expression between ethical theism and naturalistic pantheism[3]. He is careful to correct what seems to him a false inference from the language of Cicero when the outermost globe or sphere of the world is described as itself the highest God. This, he says, must be understood only in relation to the lower spheres,

[1] i. 16, 9: "nam quando homo, nisi quem doctrina philosophiae supra hominem, immo vere hominem fecit, suspicari potest stellam unam omni terra esse maiorem, cum vulgo singulae vix facis unius flammam aequare posse videantur?"

[2] i. 17, 9.

[3] Cf. Sen. *Nat. Quaest.* i. Praef. 13: "quid est deus? mens universi. quid est deus? quod vides totum et quod non vides totum." Lucan follows this in the well-known line: "Iuppiter est, quodcumque vides, quodcumque moveris" (*Pharsalia*, IX. 580).

which it encloses. The highest God, the First Cause, is not the world or a part of it, but produces the intellect from which the soul proceeds that fabricates the body of the universe[1]. With the God of this generalised theism he does not identify the deities of whom, in the *Saturnalia*, he has traced the cosmic origin. Immediately after the summary just cited, he goes on to interpret Jupiter not as the highest God but as the heaven, and Juno as the air[2]. Returning to astronomy, he adds that some think that all the stars except the sun and moon and the five called wandering stars are fixed in the heaven and simply revolve without any change of relative position; while others hold that the so-called fixed stars also change their positions, but that human life is too short to detect their motions in that immensity. This last view he takes to be nearer the truth[3].

We find a curious example of the conflict, not of reasoning but of exact observation, with "common sense," in the elaborate proof which Macrobius finds it necessary to give that the sun and moon and the five planets have a proper motion in the opposite direction to the revolution of the heaven, that is, from west to east. Not only by those without knowledge of letters, he says, but by many who have been duly instructed, the attribution of such a motion to those seven globes

[1] i. 17, 12: "quod autem hunc istum *extimum globum*, qui ita volvitur, *summum deum* vocavit, non ita accipiendum est, ut ipse prima causa et deus ille omnipotentissimus aestimetur: cum globus ipse, quod caelum est, animae sit fabrica, anima ex mente processit, mens ex deo, qui vere summus est, procreata sit."

[2] i. 17, 15: "est autem Iuno aer, et dicitur soror, quia isdem seminibus, quibus caelum, etiam aer procreatus est, coniunx, quia aer subiectus est caelo."

[3] i. 17, 16.

is judged monstrous and abhorrent to faith[1]. In the argument we can still feel the enthusiasm inspired by the first discoveries of an order in nature not immediately obvious. Julian, still more enthusiastically, relates how, as a child and without having been taught anything of astronomy, he detected, in the assiduous watching of the sky to which he was given, the motion of the moon in a direction contrary to that of the whole[2].

In his expositions of astronomical science, Macrobius on the whole keeps clear of astrology; but he has a word on the book of Plotinus entitled, in the Latin translation which then existed, *Si faciunt astra*[3]. He gives a correct account of the concession made, that, while no effect on human destiny comes from the action of the stars, certain conjunctures may be signs of future events[4]; but no adequate idea is given of the destructive nature of the attack on astrological superstition. The concession was one that Plotinus could not help making as a consequence of the doctrine, taken over from the Stoic physics, that everything in the universe is in relations of "sympathy" with everything else; but it does not sum up the drift of the book. The two essential arguments are: first, that the usual view of the astrologers about "influences," maleficent or beneficent, is absurd; and, second, that whatever share anything external may have in contributing to the complex character and destiny of a human being, there is an essence of the

[1] i. 18, 2: "non solis literarum profanis sed multis quoque doctrina initiatis abhorrere a fide ac monstro simile iudicatum est."

[2] Or. IV. 131 A B: *ὥστε ἤδη καὶ τῆς σελήνης τὴν ἐναντίαν πρὸς τὸ πᾶν αὐτὸς ἀπ' ἐμαυτοῦ κίνησιν ξυνεῖδον, οὐδενί πω ξυντυχὼν τῶν τὰ τοιαῦτα φιλοσοφούντων.*

[3] Enn. II. 3: *εἰ ποιεῖ τὰ ἄστρα.*

[4] i. 19, 27.

individual with reason for its directing power, and this can and ought to be followed. Astrology, therefore, for Plotinus, is an enemy of the rational direction of human life, almost exactly as for Sextus Empiricus. This coincidence of two such different minds is really remarkable; especially as it is the one case in which Sextus puts aside his scepticism and directly reveals the "positivity" that lies behind it in him as in Hume. Just as Hume diverges from his sceptical dialectic on causation as a rational *a priori* principle, and turns that principle (whatever its origin) against the belief in miraculous interferences with the course of nature; so Sextus departs, just for one excursion, from his predetermined plan of attacking the supposed rational basis of every "liberal science" in turn and showing all to fall short of theoretical certainty. Coming to scientific astronomy, he merely says that it depends on mathematics; that the principles of mathematics have been shown to want the character of strict science; but that he has no quarrel with what observers have made out regarding the experienced order of phenomena. He will therefore say nothing about astronomy itself, sceptical attack being superfluous after the dialectical examination of geometry; but will set himself to refute the art of the "Chaldaeans," who in manifold ways injure life, pile up for us a huge superstition, and permit no action to be done in accordance with right reason[1]. The tone of indignation against the imposture of casting nativities is unmistakable. The sceptic here delivers no masked attack, but uses the language of convinced rationalism. Plotinus, on this ground, for

[1] *Adv. Math.* v. 2: *οἱ Χαλδαῖοι...ποικίλως μὲν ἐπηρεάζοντες τῷ βίῳ, μεγάλην δ' ἡμῖν ἐπιτειχίζοντες δεισιδαιμονίαν, μηδὲν δὲ ἐπιτρέποντες κατὰ τὸν ὀρθὸν λόγον ἐνεργεῖν.*

a moment joins hands with him by becoming a determined sceptic.

Continuing the astronomical discussion, Macrobius sets forth the attempts made to calculate the size of the earth and of the sun. About the dimensions of the earth, the ancient astronomers were not far wrong; but they did not come anywhere near the actual ratio of the sun's to the earth's diameter. What we notice in the general discussion is the fixation of the Aristotelian physics. The distinctions in nature of the regions above and below the moon; the necessary order of the four elements; the tendency of heavy bodies to the centre which is the earth; all this is established dogma. But so also, as against wild schemes of geography that were to be put forth in the next age, is the globular figure of the earth and the existence of antipodes.

The second book opens with a discussion of the "music of the spheres." The theory is that the sounds of the octave are produced by their motion in relation to one another; the seven below the sphere of the fixed stars moving in the opposite direction to that of the heaven[1]. Musical sound, and not noise, is produced because the motions are in certain definite numerical proportions to one another[2]. After relating how Pythagoras is said to have discovered the intervals, Macrobius goes on to discuss the use Plato makes of mathematical doctrine in the *Timaeus* to "construct" the soul of the world. Here he recapitulates the theory of the dimensions of "body," and of the production of numbers from the monad, or unity, which is their source. Plato, he says, in applying such conceptions to the soul of the world, did not mean that it has in itself anything corporeal,

[1] ii. 1, 4. [2] ii. 1, 7.

but meant to show how, through a corresponding perfection of its own, it has the power to penetrate and fill the solid body of the whole[1]. Since the soul of the world was composed on the basis of musical proportions, it must express itself by causing motions that give rise to audible music[2].

The Sirens of Plato in the Vision of Er, Macrobius interprets as the goddesses to whom are assigned the notes of the spheres. The "theologians" also, he says, referring to Hesiod, made the Muses represent the sounds of the eight spheres together with the harmony of all. Urania is the eighth, taking the sphere of the fixed stars for her portion, and Calliope is the ninth, signifying by her name the sweetness of the supreme harmony[3]. There follows the praise of music as innate even in the souls of barbarians because they too are of celestial origin. From the power of music over peoples with no rational culture, the fables of Orpheus and Amphion took their beginning[4]. And what wonder that music has such dominion among men when even some birds practise it as if by a certain discipline of art[5]. "By right therefore everything that lives falls under the power of music, since the heavenly soul by which the universe is animated took its origin from music[6]."

[1] ii. 2, 14: "Timaeus igitur Platonis in fabricanda mundi anima consilium divinitatis enuntians ait, illam per hos numeros fuisse contextam, qui et a pari et ab impari cubum, id est perfectionem soliditatis, efficiunt, non quia aliquid significaret illam habere corporeum, sed ut possit universitatem animando penetrare et mundi solidum corpus implere, per numeros soliditatis effecta est."

[2] ii. 2, 19.

[3] ii. 3, 2: "nam Καλλιόπη optimae vocis Graeca interpretatio est."

[4] ii. 3, 8. [5] ii. 3, 10.

[6] ii. 3, 11: "iure igitur musica capitur omne, quod vivit, quia caelestis anima, qua animatur universitas, originem sumpsit ex musica."

The musical intervals, according to the doctrine of Macrobius, have their proper nature only in the incorporeal soul. But are they, he goes on to ask, preserved in the body of the world? He illustrates the possible answers by citing first an attempt of Archimedes to determine a definite law for the distances of the planets[1], and then setting against this law another which was stated by some of the Platonists. Porphyry, for example, inserted it in the books by which he shed some light on the obscurities of the *Timaeus*[2]. It is worth while to learn how closely speculations that have led to real science were at first associated with philosophic fancies. The ultimate abstract form given to these, as a kind of parallelism between the soul and body of the world[3], has still something in it that appeals to the modern philosophic mind.

For leaving out much of the technical detail, Macrobius himself furnishes an excellent reason when he says that Cicero's mention of music, if followed out into all that it suggests, would lead to disquisitions without end; and to give more than is necessary is to deepen the darkness of things naturally obscure[4]. It may suffice to say that, according to the system he follows, there are, in all, nine spheres, the stationary earth at the centre being counted as one. Eight revolve, the outermost, that of the fixed stars, being the swiftest in its revolution

[1] ii. 3, 13.

[2] ii. 3, 15: "hanc Platonicorum persuasionem Porphyrius libris inseruit, quibus Timaei obscuritatibus non nihil lucis infudit."

[3] ii. 3, 15: "ita provenire concentum, cuius ratio in substantia animae contexta mundano quoque corpori, quod ab anima movetur, inserta est."

[4] ii. 4, 12: "quia in re naturaliter obscura, qui in exponendo plura, quam necesse est, superfundit, addit tenebras, non adimit densitatem."

and yielding the highest note, while that of the moon yields the deepest. The seven planetary spheres, from Saturn to the moon, have a motion from west to east, opposite, as has been said, to the revolution of the heaven. Though eight spheres revolve, there are only seven notes, Mercury and Venus having orbits of like time, in which they follow the sun as satellites[1]; so that their force, expressed in their note, is the same[2].

In the instruction given on terrestrial geography, the characters of the zones are exaggerated both by Cicero and by Macrobius, who follows him in describing the frigid and the torrid zones as uninhabitable. Firmly maintaining, as he does against the less enlightened, the existence of antipodes, that is, inhabitants of the southern temperate zone, he yet holds that there is no way by which we can obtain direct knowledge of them or they of us. Such impassable barriers between the inhabitable parts of the earth are used by him, after Cicero, to show the limitations of fame in space. Similarly, he carries forward the argument from the necessity, to which the earth is subject, of alternate deluges and conflagrations, to prove its limitations in time even in the same region. The moral, as in Scipio's Dream itself, is that virtue must not be practised for fame as a reward.

The catastrophic view adopted by Macrobius presents some interesting variations from that which we find in Seneca. For the Stoic, the destruction of the human

[1] Julian speaks of the planets in general as circling in dance about the sun as king (περὶ αὐτὸν ὥσπερ βασιλέα χορεύοντες). See Or. IV. 135 A B, 146 C D.

[2] Hence Cicero says: "illi autem octo cursus, in quibus eadem vis est duorum, septem efficiunt distinctos intervallis sonos, qui numerus rerum omnium fere nodus est" (*Comm.* ii. 4, 9).

race at the end of each cataclysm or world-conflagration is absolute. Though regarded as being, like everything else, the outcome of natural law[1], it has very much the effect of a "dies irae." "Unus humanum genus condet dies[2]." That is the end of the progress to which, in our own world-period, Seneca can assign no limits; and in every new period the seeds of dissolution will destroy the renewed innocence of man's beginnings and prepare for the endurance of the final catastrophe that fate always has in store. Without expressly discussing this dogma of the Stoics, Macrobius effects a change in the outlook by returning to the less symmetrical theory of cycles stated in a tentative way by Plato and Aristotle.

Many of the ancients, as we know, theorised quite soundly on progress as far as it had gone. Aeschylus and Lucretius traced human civilisation to rude and savage beginnings. Before Seneca the author of the *Epinomis*, and after him Celsus and Julian, briefly stated a kind of "law of progress" in the sciences and arts from the Oriental to the Hellenic world. What prevented thinkers in later antiquity from going further was not want of generalising power. Seneca's forecast in the seventh book of the *Naturales Questiones* is as remarkable in its way as Bacon's previsions of modern progress. They were stopped by the true sense that their own civilisation was in spirit and in originality running down. Macrobius, though coming so late, is not one in whom this sense is most oppressive. He seems inclined, from study of the facts, to look for continuous development; and finally decides that there must be discontinuity only on the ground of that which seems to him the most authorised philosophical teaching.

[1] *Ratio, lex, iura naturae.*

[2] *Nat. Quaest.* iii. 29, 9.

Who, he asks, would not infer from the absence of even any Greek history of important events more than two thousand years ago (say, beyond Ninus) that the world some time began? That some nations have so lately received from others improvements in civilisation, as for example the Gauls have received the culture of the vine and olive; and that there are still nations ignorant of many improvements known to us; similarly suggests a beginning. Yet philosophy teaches that the world always existed; being framed indeed by a God, but not from a beginning in time[1]. The solution he arrives at is that the alternate deluges and conflagrations do not affect the whole earth or sweep away the whole of mankind[2]. Thus Egypt, as Plato recognises in the *Timaeus*, has in its monuments and writings an exceptionally long record. Human life, therefore, does not take a series of absolutely new beginnings: certain parts of the earth always survive as a seed-plot of the new.

This was no doubt the most reasonable solution at the time. How could any one foresee that the whole state of the question would be transformed by the return of science to a cosmogony remotely resembling that of an early philosophic poet like Empedocles? For the long vistas of evolution through the ages before there was earth or air or heaven, as Aristophanes put it in his parody of such cosmogonies[3], general consent had substituted the carefully limited imagination of the

[1] ii. 10, 9: "haec omnia videntur aeternitati rerum repugnare, dum opinari nos faciunt, certo mundi principio paulatim singula quaeque coepisse. sed mundum quidem fuisse semper philosophia auctor est conditore quidem deo, sed non ex tempore."

[2] ii. 10, 14: "numquam tamen seu eluvio seu exustio omnes terras aut omne hominum genus vel omnino operit vel penitus exurit."

[3] *Aves*, 694.

"great year" or "year of the world," at the end of which all the stars shall be in the same relative positions as at the beginning. Of this the estimate mentioned by Macrobius is 15,000 solar years[1]. His own repeated suggestion about movements of the fixed stars[2] ought to have made this seem impossibly modest; and, as a matter of fact, ancient mathematical astronomy was sufficiently developed to prove all the attempts made to determine the period of the great year a failure. Not till Laplace, however, was a decisive step taken forward on the ground of science.

To do justice to the thinkers of the age in which Macrobius lived, we must turn to the real progress made in metaphysics and secured for the future. And we must note, as one incident of this, that the fundamental principle of all physical science was not allowed to be forgotten. Cicero having made the elder Scipio describe the world as "in some part mortal," like the "fragile body" of man, Macrobius corrects the looser literary mode of expression of the orator from Plotinus, whose metaphysical doctrine had for corollary that there must be something perdurable in the material world as such. To use a phrase like that of Cicero, Macrobius observes, is to bend a little too much to common opinion. As Plotinus was careful to show, no part of the world is mortal when considered in its elements[3].

In the chapter where this occurs, Macrobius admirably characterises the style of Plotinus by the phrase "copiosa rerum densitas[4]." No one who had not read Plotinus himself as well as Porphyry could have struck out a phrase of such Latin brevity to sum up what

[1] ii. 11, 11. [2] ii. 11, 9; cf. i. 17, 16.
[3] ii. 12, 12–16. [4] ii. 12, 8.

Porphyry says, though not diffusely, yet in more words[1].

On metaphysics, Macrobius gives us here a technical discussion which he expressly declares to be compiled from other writers. He points out first that the argument in Cicero for the immortality of the soul is literally taken over from Plato's *Phaedrus:* the soul, being the principle of motion, must, as a principle, and so having no origin, be immortal. Then he proceeds to translate a series of arguments from Aristotle against ascribing motion to the soul itself[2]. Disclaiming what he says would be the presumption of opposing Aristotle or coming to the rescue of Plato by reasonings of his own, he tells us that he has collected into one body the arguments of the Platonists in defence of their master; adding anything that it was not unbecoming for him to venture in thought or expression after them.

This controversy, as we know from Proclus, continued till his time. Aristotle's criticisms of Plato he considers to have been adequately refuted by earlier members of the school—no doubt the writers of whom Macrobius makes use; but he found it still necessary to write a little book of his own. This has not been preserved, but its arguments are recalled in the Commentary on the *Timaeus.* A brief summary, based on Macrobius, but giving also the special points made by Proclus, will show that the doctrine of the Neo-Platonists themselves was quite untouched by Aristotle's criticism; though that criticism may have helped to show them how to find

[1] *Vita Plotini*, 14.

[2] The commentators have noted that these are not to be found in Aristotle in the order followed by Macrobius: see the tractates of Petit and Schedler cited above.

a more exact technical expression for their thought than was to be found in the language of Plato.

The objection of Aristotle is to the term "self-moved" as applied to the soul. What he denies is that the soul "moves itself": this seems to him to imply motion in space. The leading argument in Macrobius is that the intention in the term "self-moved" is simply to deny that the soul is moved either from outside or from within as one thing is moved by another[1]. Things, it is acutely put, do not altogether conform to Aristotle's distinctions. There is nothing that "is moved and does not move." Anything that is moved can set in motion something else. And so there is no proof that at the other extreme there must be an "unmoved mover"[2]. The beginning of motion, according to Aristotle, cannot itself move. This is quite wrong: beginnings have already the nature of that which follows from them[3]. If it is the essence of the soul to move, then, argues the objector, it can never rest; but the body, which it moves, is sometimes quiet; this it would not be if the soul were always moving. Are we then, the answer is, to take no account of the movements of thought and sense and imagination within the soul when the body seems at rest; or of the facts of growth, digestion, secretion and so forth which prove the body to be perpetually agitated?[4] At the end we come to the definitely psychological position, that the "motion of the soul" is to be interpreted of "thoughts, joys, hopes, fears," choice of good and evil and so forth[5]. Proclus puts this in a briefer

[1] ii. 15, 22; cf. 16, 12 and 21.

[2] ii. 15, 24.

[3] ii. 16, 2–3; cf. 16, 11: "constat omne initium inesse rei, cuius est initium, et ideo quicquid in quamcumque rem ab initio suo proficiscitur, hoc in ipso initio reperitur."

[4] ii. 16, 8–9.

[5] ii. 16, 24–25.

and more generalised form when he speaks of the mental processes[1] within the soul. To the defence as given by Macrobius he adds one finer point: Plato does not apply to the soul the notion of magnitude (μέγεθος). Macrobius was content with the proof that for Plato the soul is incorporeal; though perhaps, by pressing his language, already quoted, about "mathematical body[2]," we might identify his conception of the incorporeal with that of the unextended.

The closing pages of the Commentary recapitulate the advice given in the dream as to the way of return from life on earth to life in heaven. Heaven, as in the Platonic myth, is the original place of souls, from which they have fallen or been sent by some destiny. Those that attach themselves too much to things on earth have to wander for many ages before they return. Scipio is therefore told to practise virtue in administering the State, and, as an aid, to abstract himself from the body by a contemplative attitude to the world outside. In the disquisition that follows, an apparently equal place is allotted to the patriot-statesmen with no turn for contemplation, of whom Romulus is taken as the type, to the men of contemplation with no fitness for action, like Pythagoras, and to those that have combined both lives, such as Lycurgus and Solon among the Greeks, and among the Romans Numa and the two Catos[3]. Of those devoted entirely to leisured wisdom, Macrobius says, Greece has borne many, but the kind has been

[1] The exact phrase is τῶν μεταβατικῶν νοήσεων. See *Comm. in Tim.* ed. E. Diehl, ii. 279.

[2] i. 6, 35. See above, p. 60.

[3] We must think here of the elder Cato as he appears in the *De Senectute*. The historical old Cato the Censor cannot be classed among the friends of philosophy.

unknown to Rome. And in fact, he himself, whatever his origin by race, belongs distinctly to the series of the Roman philosophers. We know just enough of him to class him with Cicero, Seneca and Boethius, as one of those who combined the two lives. Less is known of him than of these; indeed nothing except the titles that prove him to have held some administrative post and the two or three circumstances that he tells us about himself; and perhaps it was the final predominance of contemplation in the soul of this "vir clarissimus et illustris" that saved him from the violent end to which a public life brought all the others, as it had brought Scipio before them.

IV

CONCLUSION

For science and letters, the value of the two works of Macrobius to an age that was to dawn long after is not easy to exaggerate. The elements of sound comparative criticism in the *Saturnalia*, and of sound astronomical science in the Commentary on Cicero, are to modern readers so familiar that the difficulty now is to see the importance of keeping them alive for a thousand years. The astonishing thing about that immense lapse is, as Gibbon said, not that so much was lost, but that we have been so fortunate in what has been preserved. To the mere persistence, through a few compendia, of the knowledge that the earth is a globe, Europe owed the discovery of the New World. The astronomical and geographical science in Macrobius alone was sufficient to furnish a basis for Columbus when the passion for exploration and discovery had been reawakened, as it was in the fifteenth century. When speculative science began again in the next century, the orthodox astronomy of the ancients no longer sufficed; but even then a basis had still to be found in antiquity. Copernicus had to put himself under the protection of the great name of Pythagoras to get even the beginnings of a hearing for his renewed heliocentric doctrine against the appeal to the traditional authority of Aristotle. And, though Macrobius is not one of the writers who preserved the record of early heliocentric ideas, probably the incidental criticism of Aristotle by the Platonists which he sympathetically set forth helped at the Renaissance to weaken the dominant Aristotelianism of the schools and so to prepare the way for all new departures.

In the Middle Ages, Macrobius was a quickening influence in another way. He furnished the schoolmen of the West with the elements of a knowledge of Platonism apart from its adaptation to Christian theology; and he helped to impress the results of the strenuous metaphysical thinking by which the ancient tradition was carried on from the third to the sixth century of the Christian era. Coming about half-way between Plotinus and the closing of the schools at Athens, he is in the very centre of this movement; and he shows himself as competent to hand on the gain in insight under the old forms as his contemporary St Augustine to appropriate it under the new[1].

It is quite possible for a trained mind in the twentieth century to adopt a worse philosophy than that which was expounded by Macrobius at the end of the fourth. For at present an increase in the subtlety of mathematics has led to a renewal of the ambition to explain man himself from the elements into which he has analysed the physical universe of which his organism is a part. Now in the age of Macrobius metaphysical thought had definitely succeeded in proving the unique character of "soul," "mind," or whatever we choose to call that which cannot be exhausted by any possible account of the order of things taken by common sense to be real and external. The attempt to explain thought, or even perception, as a modification of body or brain or of some air or finer "spirit" running through it had been proved

[1] Augustine calls his own procedure borrowing "the gold of the Egyptians" (Exod. xi. 2; xii. 35–36).

once for all to be fallacious. The result is that even now, without aid from modern idealism, the reasonings of Plotinus remain sufficient to overthrow every system of pure mechanism that may present itself as a philosophy of the universe. Yet the manipulation of formulae is so easily mistaken for thinking about realities that every increase in their power to deal with the subtleties of the external world raises again in some minds the illusory imagination that the time will come when its changes of collocation will be proved to be all, and the understanding or perception of them a superfluous appearance or accident.

Plotinus is supposed, not without reason, to be a difficult philosopher; and there is one section of his work—the books on the Categories—which I have expressed agreement with Dean Inge in finding "one of the most obscure and least attractive parts of the Enneads[1]." Yet I venture to assert that, in these on the whole repellent books, there are passages which, taken simply by themselves, prove in advance the futility of all modern, as of all ancient, attempts to reach the explanation of mind from the outside. And in clearness they leave nothing to be desired; though I must confess that to me they seem to stand out from the tangled subject-matter of the first three books of the sixth Ennead as the occasional bright sentences in the last two books of Aristotle's *Metaphysics* stand out from the discussion of the theory of numbers.

The most amazing thing of all, says Plotinus, is that those who trust the senses for knowledge of each thing, assert that that is real being which cannot be seized

[1] *The Hibbert Journal*, April, 1919, p. 548.

by sense[1]. Does this lose any of its force when for the hard atoms of Epicurus or the continuous corporeal substance supposed by the Stoics to underlie the four transformable elements, we substitute the electrons or ether of modern physics? That the theories of physics become more "idealistic" by their subtlety, as some imagine, I regard indeed only as another fallacy. Ether and electrons, if they are physical existents, are matter or body[2], and not something intermediate between body and mind. I lay no stress on the fineness of the particles or the medium, but only contend that the argument of the metaphysician has lost none of its force through the progress of physical theory.

The only way in which this argument could be turned is by asserting, as Democritus did in distinction from his successors, that the criterion of reality is reason as against the senses. This, however, though it was plausible at the time of the vague early psychology and theory of knowledge, would not do at all for a materialist in the period of more developed thinking. The "reason" appealed to is evidently the reason of the individual thinker; and how can he think it as actually consisting in the distribution of the material particles that are, according to his doctrine, the true underlying reality? It was easier to suppose knowledge of the external given immediately by sense. Plotinus has in fact both suggested and met in advance this possible reversion of the materialist from empiricism to rationalism. One who reduces all qualitative change to change of collocation

[1] Enn. VI. 1, 28: *πάντων τε θαυμαστότατον τὸ τῇ αἰσθήσει πιστουμένους ἕκαστα τὸ μὴ τῇ αἰσθήσει ἁλωτὸν τίθεσθαι ὄν.*

[2] If the ancient distinction between matter and body should ever be revived, the ether would have to be called "matter" and the electrons "first bodies."

(as Democritus tried to do) must suppose the emergent quality to be nothing at all. All that truly exists must be simply elements quantitatively distinguishable, brought nearer to one another or separated. But how can mental synthesis (illustrated for example in learning and teaching) consist in aggregations of such elements?[1]

These arguments, it seems to me, show less symbolically and more directly than we can do it by means of our terms "object" and "subject," the impossibility of explaining what is essential in mind from the subtlest processes in things supposed quantitatively distinguishable into parts external to one another. This is not done by setting another kind of "substance" against the substance of bodies. What we find is thought becoming aware of the unique character of all that is mental. When this has been made quite clear, the doctrines that try to explain mind from external things (or, still more subtly, from mathematical quantities) become in their turn extremely baffling. We hesitate to deal with them because we are not sure what they are supposed to mean. Intellectual clearness has passed over from the side of physics to that of metaphysics.

At present the conjecture may perhaps be forgiven that some of the new mathematical developments which have been brought into relation with metaphysics are not yet science, but only, as Berkeley allowed that the calculus in his time might be, a knack for getting at results. Some philosophical mathematician may, we are

[1] Enn. VI. 3, 25: *εἰ γὰρ πᾶσαν ἀλλοίωσιν, ἣν λέγομεν κατὰ ποιότητα μεταβολήν, σύγκρισιν καὶ διάκρισιν λέγοι, τὸ γινόμενον οὐδέν ἐστιν, ἀλλὰ ἐγγὺς κείμενα καὶ διεστῶτα. ἔπειτα τὸ μανθάνειν καὶ τὸ διδάσκεσθαι πῶς συγκρίσεις;*

led to hope by the past history of science, clear up the new mysteries as De Morgan cleared up those of the calculus[1]. When this is done, it must evidently be by putting the whole process into terms of intellect, in which the formulae can, whenever we like, be referred to the relations between the imagined measurements or countings that they represent. Thus may the mathematician (if he needs this insight) be brought to see that, powerful as his science is, the quantities with which it deals will never explain himself—that is, his mind.

When metaphysical thought has gone so far, however, there remains the problem of carrying over what is distinctively, in Hume's phrase, one of the "abstract and profound philosophies" into a relatively "easy philosophy." Macrobius partly succeeded in doing this; and, in the history of the human race, nothing is of more practical importance than such a transformation may be. Of course it will never be possible to have done once for all with the "abstruse philosophy," as Hume ironically suggested at the opening of the *Inquiry*. We can imagine how he would have smiled at his own invitation to his readers if he could have read his successor, Kant. The reward in store for those who might read Hume in the hope, after so much mental labour, to be rid of "metaphysics" for ever, was to find themselves confronted with the *Critique of Pure Reason*! Still, if philosophy is to produce an effect on the world, it must get itself expressed in a form more available than that

[1] I have been glad to see that Prof. A. E. Taylor, who has drawn attention recently to the importance of De Morgan's work, has a good word to say even for Hobbes's criticisms of "the nascent calculus." "Hobbes's objection to the infinitesimal was, in fact, logically sound." (*Mind*, N.S., April, 1922, p. 209.)

of Hume's *Treatise* or Kant's *Critique*. As an attempt at a transition to an easier philosophy, Hume's *Inquiry* was justified; but, so far, the ancients have had more success in this kind than the moderns. Even for the modern world, perhaps Cicero and Seneca and Plutarch have done more to furnish a popular philosophy that is still philosophy than any among its own writers who have been at once philosophers and men of letters.

This may be best seen by considering the eighteenth century, the age when educated Europe had again, for the first time since the later period of antiquity, a kind of philosophical outlook that was fairly general and did not require much technical accomplishment. Now the ancients at that time were still the most authorised teachers because in a manner they stood above party. Those who were occupied in criticising by implication the inherited religious order, and those who defended it, alike to a large extent formed themselves ethically on the ancient moralists and appealed to them. And those appealed to were chiefly the representatives of what Hume calls "the easy philosophy." We may see this in Gibbon's decided preference of Cicero to Aristotle; whose fame indeed, as Hume said, in that age seemed to be "utterly decayed." From this diffused influence of philosophy came much of what was best in the eighteenth century. In Gibbon himself, whatever may be said to his disadvantage, we feel the genuinely philosophical serenity of his attitude of detachment towards the struggle for power and wealth among the practical leaders of mankind. Devotion to knowledge and literature, as against practical ambition, was without the least affectation his own voluntary choice. On the other hand, he is wanting in the sense of what Schopenhauer called the need of mankind for metaphysics. His one prejudice may be said to be a dislike for every kind of "enthusiasm"; and, as Plato had shown, the metaphysical philosopher is necessarily an enthusiast. Thus he was misled regarding the latest philosophy of antiquity. In a way that can only be explained by a partial neglect to study the thought of the ages he dealt with when it had no visible and tangible influence on action, he describes the latest pagans as "fanatical polytheists." Perhaps the neglect was justifiable when the mass of detail with which he was directly concerned was so gigantic; for the great historian might have read all the philosophical treatises of the Neo-Platonists without gleaning the materials for a single note on the facts of the time; but a Christian theologian like Cudworth, whose work he knew, had corrected in advance his error about Julian. And the case of Julian was that of all his educated pagan contemporaries, who were formally as much monotheists as the Jews or Christians. If they and their party, as represented still among the contemporaries of Macrobius, continued to find Hellenic more congenial than Judaic myth, it might seem that Gibbon ought to have sympathised with them.

Gibbon was, however, too "positive" to care much about play with myth of any kind. The preference he actually shows is for the more sober philosophical writers, whether nominally pagan or Christian. And personally, as well as by the influence of his time, he had no taste for the "accurate and abstract" philosophy which Hume confessed was delightful to him while he affected to think it futile. Hence Boethius is treated with more respect than his Greek masters precisely because in the *De Consolatione Philosophiae* he does not follow them in their abstruser disquisitions, but keeps his thought within the limits of what appeals to cultivated readers in general. Yet Gibbon's age was succeeded by another which in turn was inclined to depreciate everything of this kind as mere "popular philosophy"; and so nearly all serious philosophising has since become highly technical. This is in some ways unfortunate for philosophy and for literature and for life. If we had now a literary philosophy that could make a still wider appeal than that of the cosmopolitan period of the Graeco-Roman world, the hope for modern civilisation would be indefinitely increased. But a condition is that it must not, in becoming popular, cease to be metaphysical. Macrobius and Boethius avoided this danger; and there was enough left in them of the "accurate and abstract" philosophy of the Greeks to retain its stimulating power for the whole of the Middle Age. When the Greeks themselves returned, their Roman disciples could no longer remain what they had been for the world; but even now, as a stimulus of hope for the future, we cannot do better than take a hint from Macrobius and turn back to the one philosopher who by universal consent stands above the distinction between the "abstruse" and the "easy" philosophy. Macrobius, expressing the fundamental conviction of his own school, declares the arguments of Plato's *Phaedo* to be of demonstrative force. And of no dialogue more than of the *Phaedo* can it be said that it retains to this day all its power as literature. Let us then, as an experiment in bringing together the two modes of treating philosophy, try to find out, in the light of the decidedly abstruse thinking of Plato's successors, what intellectual validity his arguments may retain beneath their consummate literary form.

We must not let this literary form become a cause of deception. Plato seems to stop himself again and again in writing beautifully, and turn back resolutely to argument, willing as the reader might be to acquiesce in the pleasure given by rhetoric from a position taken as already achieved. And to modern readers the arguments themselves, in spite of their far more attractive literary form, are less readily accessible as serious attempts at proof than those of the Neo-Platonic school. The later ancients found a slight archaism in the language of Plato; and we find some archaism in his thought as compared with that of his successors.

This becomes perceptible when we meet with the assertion that souls come from the dead and go to the dead. Obviously this implies some kind of indestructibility in that which thinks or feels or perceives. But does it mean that indestructible individual souls go away and return, or that there is a general fund of "soul" out of which they emerge and into which they are reabsorbed? And what is it that persists? Is it thought only, or perception also? And is the "memory" by which thought is said to be revived from one life to another to be taken literally, or is it semi-mythical?

The view at which I have arrived is this. Plato's doctrine is already fundamentally the same as that of Plotinus and Proclus. There is a limited number of individual souls, existing necessarily and not by accident[1]; and that which is certainly immortal in each is

[1] The element of pluralism developed further by Proclus is definitely present already in Plotinus. See Enn. vi. 2, 8: *πλείω μὲν δὴ λέγομεν εἶναι καὶ οὐ κατὰ τύχην πλείω.* Cf. 15: *καὶ ταὐτὸν δὲ*

rational thought. I hold also that Proclus, with the general "orthodox" view both of antiquity and of the Middle Ages, was justified in ascribing to Aristotle the belief that the "separable intellect" is an individually immortal principle. Alexander of Aphrodisias, who said that the rational principle in all mankind is the Deity, and Averroes, who said that it is the general human intellect as a divine emanation, were putting forward original doctrines under the authority of Aristotle. For Aristotle, as for his master Plato, there was an individual intellect, not due to an accidental conjuncture of a general intellect with a particular organism; though he rejected, at least as dogma, belief in the persistence of memory and perception from one life to another. Plotinus, while explaining the Platonic reminiscence as a half-mythical expression of the true doctrine of "innate ideas," yet, by an original psychological development, argued for the persistence of memory, though not of perception. About the exact position of Proclus on memory we cannot be quite sure; nor do I think that we can be sure about the position of Plato himself.

Whether we take reminiscence literally or not, the argument in the *Phaedo* from the nature of rational knowledge evidently implies that the souls are individual. An argument that to know is really to know again, to "recognise," and therefore in some sense to remember, would not have the least relevance to a doctrine like the naturalism—rather poetically expressed, as his reporter said—of Anaximander, according to which the emergence of one separate existence is an "injustice" to the others, and has to be expiated by reabsorption

καὶ θάτερον οὐχ ὕστερα, ὅτι μὴ ὕστερον ἐγένετο πολλά, ἀλλ' ἦν ὅπερ ἦν ἓν πολλά.

into the infinite[1]. The descent of the soul, as imagined by Plato, is from a society of individual souls living a divine life together, of which some grow weary. Removing the imaginative elements, we can put the argument in this form. Rational knowledge, for example of geometry, is inexplicable without principles in the mind, called forth by experience of the particulars of sense, but not contained in the sum of these: therefore the mind is not a resultant of the particulars of sensible experience, but was before the series of them began. Now this evidently implies that the mind is something enduring by itself, and not a mere temporary modification of the whole.

The argument for immortality treated in the *Phaedo* as finally valid is that the soul cannot die, because it "participates in the idea of life." This at first sight looks too much a technical argument within a particular school to appeal to hearers outside that school: but let us put it in this way. The body can die, that is, lose its internal order and be broken up into parts and dispersed, without ceasing to be body. Nothing of corporeal kind is destroyed. Can the soul—the total of a mental life—be similarly broken up and dispersed without ceasing to be soul? Have we any knowledge (as we have in the case of body) of aggregates from which the elements into which we can analyse it are collected, and into which they can return without loss? If we cannot here find a correspondence with body, then to say that "the soul dies" is to say that something of a certain

[1] Diels, *Fragmente der Vorsokratiker*, I. 2nd ed. p. 13: *ἐξ ὧν δὲ ἡ γένεσίς ἐστι τοῖς οὖσι, καὶ τὴν φθορὰν εἰς ταῦτα γίνεσθαι κατὰ τὸ χρεών· διδόναι γὰρ αὐτὰ δίκην καὶ τίσιν ἀλλήλοις τῆς ἀδικίας κατὰ τὴν τοῦ χρόνου τάξιν.*

kind has simply come into being from nothing and again ceased to be. What Plato meant to say is that this is inconsistent with the conditions of coherent thought about soul, as the physical philosophers had found it to be with the conditions of thought about body.

But of course what the more subtle materialists denied was that that whole of mental life called the soul is anything but a modification of the body dependent on the coexistence of its parts in certain postures to one another. These postures are always being modified, and when a certain kind of modification arrives in the course of everlasting motion, that which was said to be living is said to be dead. There is no question of "the soul" as a real existence other than a kind of modification of body. It is with this subtle form of materialism that Plato deals. The less subtle form, which treated soul as a kind of body with an aptitude through its mobility for becoming sensitive and arriving at thought, though it was commoner and had a long future, he ignored. The doctrine which he treats in the *Phaedo* as peculiarly formidable to believers in immortality had been arrived at within the Pythagorean school as a development of the first attempt at thoroughgoing explanation of everything on the lines of mathematical physics. Vague as it is in outline, it leaves nothing in principle for the subtlest modern materialists to add. The soul, said these Pythagoreans, is "the harmony of the body." It can no more exist apart from the body than the tune can exist when the lyre has been broken. The reply of Plato has been thought weaker than the materialist's case as stated by him; but we need only put it in modern terms to see that it is still quite valid. The soul, he replies, is itself capable of harmony; it can be, as a soul, harmonised or not; but there cannot be a harmony of a harmony; and so, that account of the soul does not succeed in describing it as we know it. Now let us apply this to a modern statement equivalent to that of the ancient materialists. The saying was attributed to Cabanis that "the brain secretes thought as the liver secretes bile." This is one of the things that were never said quite so epigrammatically by the persons to whom they were ascribed[1]; but Cabanis did apparently say that the brain "*en quelque sorte* digests impressions" and "performs organically the secretion of thought[2]." To those assertions a reply exactly equivalent to that of Plato can be made. There is, as a fact, "thinking on thought." Is there "digestion of digestive process" or "secretion of secretive process"? Clearly the analogy fails. Mind or soul is unique. It cannot even be described in terms that run parallel with a description of the organism or its parts.

Of course we cannot be finally confident, any more than Plato could, that we have got hold of the truth

[1] We know from Plutarch that in antiquity the saying "God geometrises" (ὁ θεὸς γεωμετρεῖ) was ascribed to Plato, but that students of his writings knew that it was not there. William of Ockham, we have learnt recently, nowhere said in so many words, *Entia non sunt multiplicanda praeter necessitatem*. That Numenius described Plato as "an Attic Moses" has been doubted. It has long been known that Julian did not say *Vicisti, Galilaee*, and that Kosciuszko did not say *Finis Poloniae*.

Numenius, however, did allude to the Hebrew books (Gen. i. 2; see Porphyry, *De Antro Nympharum*, c. 10); and it would be very plausible, if, after all, the historical Longinus wrote the treatise *On the Sublime*, to attribute his reference to the Hebrew legislator to the influence of Numenius, whom we know that he had studied.

[2] See Croom Robertson's *Philosophical Remains* ("The Ideologists"), p. 478, where, however, these expressions are described as "unguarded," and not representing the deeper thought of Cabanis, who "shows himself well aware of the unique import of conscious sensibility."

about our destiny in any sense that interests our feelings. He represents Socrates as desiring this confidence, but dependent finally on argument, not intuition; and modern philosophers cannot follow a better example than his of arguing to the last. That, in fact, is their business in life. Of one thing, however, we can be as sure as Plato's successors of the sceptical Academy were: that the critical philosophy set going in their school was adequate to destroy by purely intellectual argument every system of dogmatism about the external world that took it as being, prior to philosophical thought, a known reality. Historically, the sceptics, Academic and other, held the position safely against materialist dogmatism till a new constructive idealism could arise. So far, in modern times, nothing so durable has appeared as the system of Neo-Platonism. What we need, in order to go beyond it, is not now, it seems to me, greater caution, but rather the resolution to emulate the ancients in audacity, and not refuse to put any questions about the universe or about human or individual destiny that the subtlest thought aided by the most wide-ranging imagination can conceive. Sobriety is good in so far as it excludes known impossibilities of thought; but, when rival possibilities present themselves, there is not even a presumption that the more sober view will turn out right. What could be more plausible in the eighteenth century than the argument that the most strictly bounded outline of cosmogony and of human history was likely to be the most true, as being the most contrary to national vanity and to the general passion of mankind for wonders? Yet nothing was further from the truth. The tropical reverie of India came nearer, in its lavish profusion of aeons, to the form of past evolution, than the limited schemes ranging through a few thousand years. To correspond, metaphysical imagination has had a freer course in India than in Europe. Perhaps it will turn out that this has not spent itself in vain; for we have now scholars to interpret it to us with exactitude. We must, indeed, preserve our sobriety so far as not to lose ourselves in reverie; and for this Europe has provided the means. We are well weighted with ascertained science, and we have our "accurate and abstract" philosophies. But the essential thing seems to be, not to care too much for results. This we can still learn from the ancients, even from those who, like Macrobius, came near the end. If we can learn the lesson in philosophy as in science, then, whatever may be the truth about our personal being, we may rest in the confidence that thought will go on in the future of the world as in the past. The sometime derided "metaphysical instinct of the Aryan race," having persisted in spite of so many alien forces, will last, we may be sure, as long as humanity.

INDEX

For EU product safety concerns, contact us at Calle de José Abascal, 56–1°,
28003 Madrid, Spain or eugpsr@cambridge.org.

www.ingramcontent.com/pod-product-compliance
Ingram Content Group UK Ltd.
Pitfield, Milton Keynes, MK11 3LW, UK
UKHW020312140625
459647UK00018B/1840

* 9 7 8 1 1 0 7 4 5 0 9 7 4 *